ASIAN HERITAGE CHEFS IN WHITE HOUSE HISTORY

Cooking to the President's Taste

To Alice,

Enjoy this taste of presidential history!

Adrian Miller
1/22/26

ASIAN HERITAGE CHEFS IN WHITE HOUSE HISTORY

Cooking to the President's Taste

ADRIAN MILLER AND DEBORAH CHANG

THE **WHITE HOUSE** *HISTORICAL ASSOCIATION*

THE WHITE HOUSE HISTORICAL ASSOCIATION

The White House Historical Association is a nonprofit educational association founded in 1961 for the purpose of enhancing the understanding, appreciation, and enjoyment of the Executive Mansion. All proceeds from the sale of the Association's books and products are used to fund the acquisition of historic furnishings and art work for the permanent White House Collection, assist in the preservation of public rooms, and further its educational mission.

BOARD OF DIRECTORS

John F. W. Rogers, *Chairman*

Teresa Carlson, *Vice Chairperson*

Gregory W. Wendt, *Treasurer*

Anita B. McBride, *Secretary*

Stewart D. McLaurin, *President*

Eula Adams, Michael Beschloss, Gahl Hodges Burt, Merylnn Carson, Jean M. Case, Ashley Dabbiere, Wayne A. I. Frederick, Deneen C. Howell, Barbara A. Perry, Nicole Sexton, Ben C. Sutton Jr., Tina Tchen

NATIONAL PARK SERVICE LIAISON: Charles F. Sams III

EX OFFICIO: Lonnie G. Bunch III, Omar Eaton-Martinez, Kaywin Feldman, Carla Hayden

DIRECTORS EMERITI: John T. Behrendt, John H. Dalton, Knight Kiplinger, Elise K. Kirk, Martha Joynt Kumar, James I. McDaniel, Robert M. McGee, Harry G. Robinson III, Ann Stock, Gail Berry West

WHITE HOUSE ENDOWMENT AND ACQUISITIONS TRUST

Frederick J. Ryan, Jr., *Chairman*

John T. Behrendt, Ashley Dabbiere, Anita B. McBride, James I. McDaniel, Barbara A. Perry, John F. W. Rogers, Tina Tchen

EDITORIAL AND PRODUCTION STAFF

Marcia Mallet Anderson, *Chief Publishing Officer*

Lauren McGwin, *Associate Vice President of Publishing*

Rebecca Durgin Kerr, *Editorial Coordinator*

Jennifer Wojeck, *Editorial and Production Manager*

Ann Hofstra Grogg, *Consulting Editor*

DESIGN

Pentagram

Copyright © 2025 White House Historical Association.

All rights reserved under international copyright conventions. No part of this book may be reproduced or utilized in any form or by any means, electronic or mechanical, including photocopying, recording, or by any information storage and retrieval system, without permission in writing from the publisher. Requests for reprint permissions should be addressed to Rights and Reproductions Manager, White House Historical Association, PO Box 27624, Washington D.C. 20038.

FIRST EDITION

10 9 8 7 6 5 4 3 2 1

Library of Congress Control Number: 2024953037

ISBN 978-1-950273-68-3

Printed in Italy

To Lee Ping Quan whose presidential yacht memoir cookbook anchored this work.

And to all the past, present, and future Asian heritage culinary professionals involved in presidential hospitality.

Contents

VIII   FOREWORD BY STEWART D. McLAURIN
X   PREFACE BY ADRIAN MILLER

History

- 2   Chefs and Stewards of Presidential Yachts
- 14   In Depth with Lee Ping Quan
- 24   Presidential Retreats and the White House Mess
- 36   At the Helm in the White House Kitchen
- 48   White House Staff Chefs and State Dinner Guest Chefs

Recipes

- 66   Introduction by Deborah Chang
- 68   Starters, Sides, Salads, and Soups
- 94   Entrées
- 112   Baked Goods and Desserts
- 140   More from Navy, Staff, and Guest Chefs

164   NOTES
167   ILLUSTRATION CREDITS
168   INDEX
170   ABOUT THE AUTHORS
172   ACKNOWLEDGMENTS

Stewart D. McLaurin visits the USS Potomac, *a one-time presidential yacht, where Chef Irineo Esperancilla once served President Franklin D. Roosevelt, March 12, 2024.*

Foreword

STEWART D. McLAURIN

PRESIDENT, WHITE HOUSE HISTORICAL ASSOCIATION

In 1962, while giving her celebrated televised tour of the White House, First Lady Jacqueline Kennedy announced, "We are going to do a book." This famous promise, first fulfilled by *The White House: An Historic Guide*, launched the scholarly publishing program of the White House Historical Association, which has since produced more than 175 titles. Each opens a window, in many cases for the first time, on the vast and rich subject of White House history. Just such a new window is opened in the pages that follow. *Asian Heritage Chefs in White House History: Cooking to the President's Taste* by Adrian Miller and Deborah Chang is an extraordinary example of the White House history that has been waiting to be discovered.

Inspired by a long-out-of-print biography of Lee Ping Quan, a Chinese-born chef who served Presidents Warren G. Harding and Calvin Coolidge on the USS *Mayflower*, author Adrian Miller decided to dig deeper. He found that the culinary history of the White House has included chefs from China, Japan, the Philippines, South Korea, and Thailand—from the nineteenth century to the present day. Miller shares their stories here, collaborating with Deborah Chang, who presents their recipes. Together Miller and Chang demonstrate that White House culinary history is not just about food. Chef Ah Loy prepared the opening luncheon for the Russo-Japanese peace negotiations that earned President Theodore Roosevelt the Nobel Peace Prize. President Franklin Roosevelt's personal chef, Irineo Esperancilla, served Winston Churchill and Joseph Stalin in Tehran during World War II. The journeys of these chefs to the kitchens of presidential yachts, retreats, and the White House and the monumental events they witnessed firsthand are not just culinary history; they are also social history, cultural history, human history, military history, and American history.

Miller explains that chefs featured on these pages are representative, not comprehensive, and there may be other stories yet to be told. He opens at sea with Chefs Ah Loy, Shiro Tsurusaki, Lee Ping Quan, and Irineo Esperancilla, voyages that take us from the Theodore Roosevelt to the Dwight D. Eisenhower presidencies. We go to Camp David and the vice president's residence with Chef Ariel De Guzman during the George H. W. Bush presidency, and then to the White House with Chefs Pedro Udo, Cristeta Comerford, Johnny Paje, Susan Limb, and Tommy Kurpradit, who have prepared meals for first families and visiting heads of state from the mid-twentieth century to the present. Miller's research is enriched by the biographies, memoirs, cookbooks, and news coverage of the early chefs, and by his own interviews with former and current White House chefs. We learn that each chef has taken a unique path to the American dream, but they share remarkable talents, a devotion to excellence, and a pride in their service.

Through Deborah Chang, who selected and shaped sixty recipes that can be made in a twenty-first-century home kitchen, we see that featured chefs specialize not only in Asian dishes but also in creative approaches to fusion cuisine, healthy choices, and American classics such as fried chicken and chocolate cream pie.

From good food to important history, there is something for everyone in this book, and I am sure Mrs. Kennedy would be pleased with this fitting addition to our books-in-print, which serve as a tangible representation of the Association's mission to enhance understanding, appreciation, and enjoyment of the historic White House, as they have from the start.

Preface
ADRIAN MILLER

In 1999, as a young lawyer, I joined the staff of President Bill Clinton's Initiative for One America, an outgrowth of his Initiative on Race. Toward the end of his presidency, I held the title of special assistant to the president. I had top-secret security clearance and had developed a growing—yet unsatiated—appetite for learning all about the history of our presidential cuisine and those who prepared it. Knowing what I now know, I wish that I had used my top-secret clearance and hung out more in the main White House Kitchen and gotten to know the cooks who prepared the meals for the first family. But, then and now, I'm not a nosy person, and I try not to venture anywhere I'm not invited. Talk about a missed opportunity! Or was it?

Ever since my own time at the White House, I have had a soft spot for delving into the rich history of the people who nourished our country's leaders. In fact, this ever-growing passion turned my career trajectory from lawyer and policy maker to telling the unsung stories of those who helped shape American cuisine.

Then, in 2015, I "met" my first Asian heritage presidential chef while researching African American presidential chefs in Denver, Colorado, my hometown.

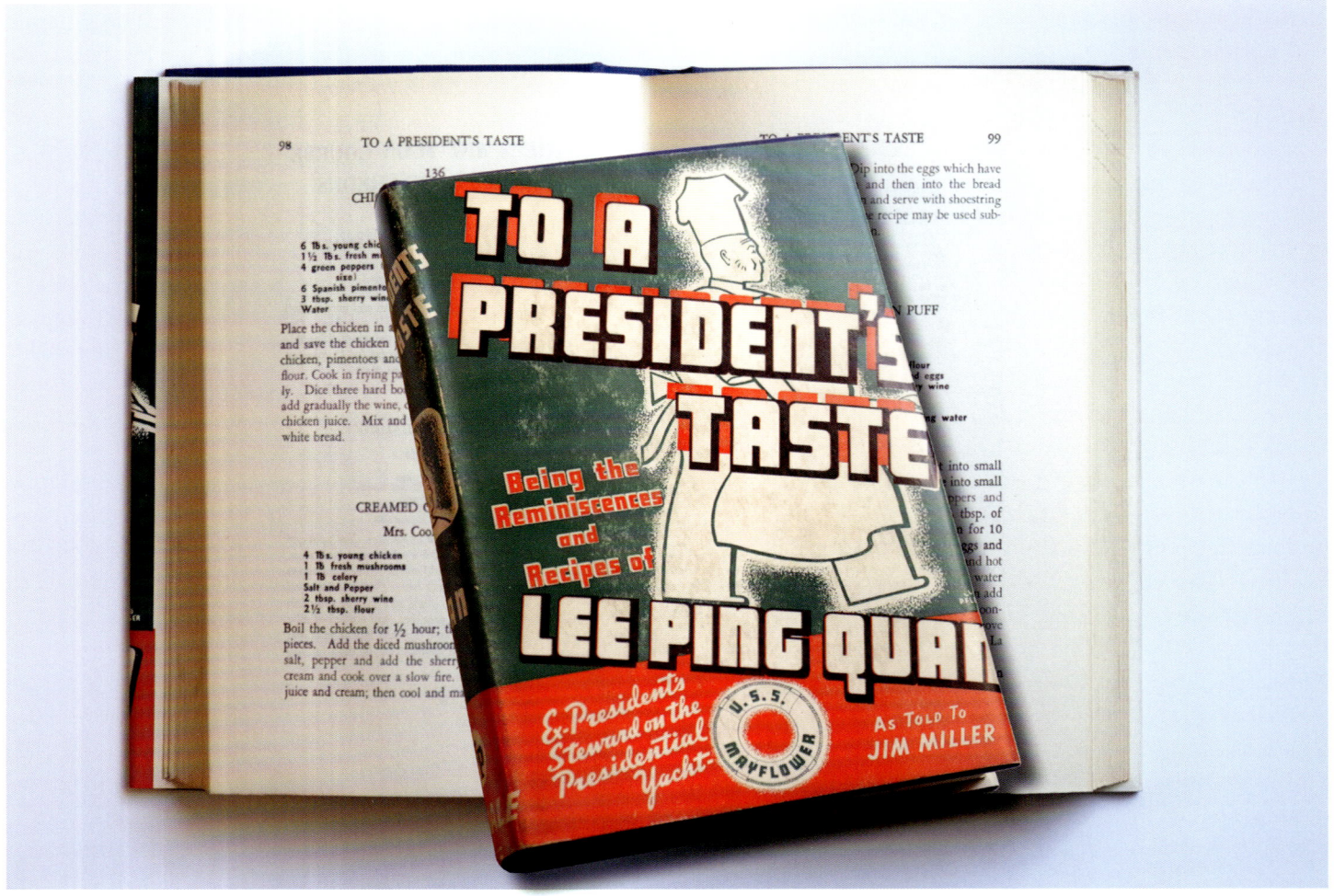

Tucked into the stacks within the University of Denver Library's Special Collections Department, I discovered the Margaret Husted Collection, which included a whopping eleven thousand culinary items. Since the library was near to where I lived, I often stopped by to explore. One day, hoping to get a hit for Black chefs in the White House, I entered "presidential" as a search term in the online catalog. To my surprise, the following entry popped up: *To a President's Taste: Being the Reminiscences and Recipes of Lee Ping Quan, Ex-President's Steward on the Presidential Yacht, U.S.S. Mayflower, As Told to Jim Miller,* published in 1939 by Rodale Press. "Sweet!" I exclaimed. Even though the book is not about a Black chef, I thought to myself, What an interesting resource.

As I leafed through the pages, I realized I had found a rare treasure. The author, Jim Miller (no relation), extensively interviewed Lee Ping Quan, giving the reader a real feel for Quan's life story and his mindset as a chef as well as his interactions with various first families. Yet Quan's book seemed to be lost to history. I immediately tried to find my own copy online and found one in good condition for $75. With my recent career change, I was so broke I couldn't justify the cost. Looking back, I should have just indulged. At the time of writing this book, a signed copy sells online for $1805.50. Sigh. While I yearned to get Quan's story out in 2015, I decided to shelve the project for a later date.

When I revisited the idea of bringing Quan's story to a larger, contemporary audience, my first thought was to go the self-publishing route and reprint the cookbook in its entirety, for pure historic value, without any changes. That was a hard sell. Then I thought of a reprint with updates to Quan's biography, adapting the recipes for a modern kitchen. As I kept researching, though, I came across more Asian heritage cooks (defined below) in presidential food service, and it seemed to me that Quan's book could be a launching point for telling the broader, and largely untold, story of these cooks. I knew I could handle the history part, but I realized that I needed someone familiar with cooking Asian food to update the recipes. Over a fantastic meal at Catch NYC, I floated the idea of teaming up on this book with my Stanford University classmate Deborah Chang, who had more recently added "culinary school graduate" to her impressive resume. In time, she agreed to the project, and we created a proposal that was ultimately accepted by the White House Historical Association.

Because so many of the presidential cooks featured in this book had varying immigration status, using "Asian American" as an identifier is imprecise. I use "Asian heritage" as an umbrella term to embrace the following countries and cultures determined by the U.S. Census Bureau:

Asian: A person having origins in any of the original peoples of the Far East, Southeast Asia, or the Indian subcontinent including, for example, Cambodia, China, India, Japan, Korea, Malaysia, Pakistan, the Philippine Islands, Thailand, and Vietnam.

Native Hawaiian or other Pacific Islander: A person having origins in any of the original peoples of Hawaii, Guam, Samoa, or other Pacific Islands.

Despite extensive outreach, I have only been able to identify presidential chefs with roots in China, Japan, the Philippines, South Korea, and Thailand. There may be more stories of presidential chefs from other parts of Asia.

This book has two parts. The first is a recap of the historical contributions and experiences of these cooks. Given the numerous Asian heritage presidential chefs that I have uncovered, what follows is a representative, rather than a comprehensive, approach. We draw out the stories of a few fascinating people who worked in a particular aspect of presidential food service as a proxy for others in that field. In chapter 1, we begin with the noncitizen immigrants who entered the U.S. Navy and were assigned to the culinary operations on presidential yachts. Chapter 2 is an in-depth focus on Lee Ping Quan that is drawn from his memoir cookbook. Chapter 3 introduces the world of cooks for presidential retreats and the White House Mess in the White House's West Wing. The White House executive chefs are the most familiar faces of presidential cooking to the broader public, and their stories are told in chapter 4. Chapter 5, the final chapter in the first part of this book, takes a look at the role Asian heritage chefs have had in more recent changes to presidential food service.

The second part of this book follows a more traditional cookbook format with selected recipes from Quan's original cookbook as well as recipes from other Asian heritage presidential cooks.

History

CHAPTER ONE

CHEFS AND STEWARDS OF PRESIDENTIAL YACHTS

Every trip Mrs. Coolidge ordered chop suey—every trip.
—AH LOY

Chef Ah Loy, 1929.

President Theodore Roosevelt with Russian and Japanese envoys aboard the USS Mayflower, *1905. Left to right, Russian diplomats Count Sergei Witte and Baron Roman Romanovich Rosen, Roosevelt, and Japanese diplomats Marquis Komura Jutarō and Baron Takahira Kogorō.*

President Theodore Roosevelt believed that September 5, 1905, would be a date long remembered for promoting harmony. Leading up to this day, he had successfully persuaded representatives from Japan and Russia to gather for peace talks, hoping to quell the rival nations' territorial ambitions in eastern Asia. Their conflict had erupted into the yearlong Russo-Japanese War and was later labeled "The First Modern War" or "World War Zero," by historians, "given the modern weapons employed, huge armies and navies engaged, and its effect on European colonialism and the international balance of power."[1] Roosevelt's proposed talks looked like a "win-win" for all sides involved. Russia was losing badly, and ending the war could help ease its own roiling domestic politics. Japan had significant leverage given its military success but was not interested in a protracted war that would drain its resources.[2] Given the political climate, President Roosevelt was confident that playing a lead role as mediator would further establish the United States as a key player on the international stage and demonstrate a potent symbol of military might during that era—the U.S. Navy.

Roosevelt also pushed for peace to curb Japanese expansionism after Japan's surprisingly decisive battles against Russia. After all, the United States had recently increased its presence in the region by taking possession of Hawaii and the Philippines. Roosevelt's combination of public overtures and back-channel communications eventually got the bitter adversaries to agree to talk and to meet in the United States, but no one wanted to endure the hot and humid late summer months in Washington, D.C. The search for a venue began but was limited to the upper East Coast, as Roosevelt did not want to be too far from his summer retreat in Oyster Bay, New York.

Portsmouth, New Hampshire, emerged as the preferred location for the talks due to the naval yard's heightened security, relative seclusion, and enhanced communications infrastructure (a new telegraph cable was nearby). It was also believed that the Japanese might encounter more racism than the Russians if the event were to be held in the more densely populated, and predominantly white, location of Newport, Rhode Island.[3] Additionally, with talks set to take place in a seaside community, Roosevelt made the unorthodox move of scheduling much of the activity aboard the U.S. Navy ships rather than in facilities on land. As a result, the USS *Dolphin* and the USS *Mayflower* became floating stages for this diplomatic drama. The *Mayflower* was described by former White House correspondent Kenneth T. Walsh as "the largest and fanciest presidential yacht."[4]

According to historian Walter Jaffee, U.S. presidential yachts date back to the mid-1800s. "Abraham Lincoln was the first president to use a yacht," he wrote. "In May 1862 Lincoln steamed down the Potomac River in the revenue cutter *Miami* to review his troops. Three years later the sidewheel paddle steamer *River Queen* was chartered for him, becoming the first vessel dedicated and maintained for a president's use." A succession of different boats followed: the USS *Despatch* (Rutherford B. Hayes in 1880); the USS *Dolphin*, an unarmed cruiser (Benjamin Harrison to Warren G. Harding); the more elegant USS *Sylph* (Theodore Roosevelt); and the USS *Mayflower* (Theodore Roosevelt to Herbert Hoover).[5]

The *Mayflower* was originally built as a private pleasure yacht in Scotland in 1896, but then the U.S. government purchased it in 1898. "On March 19 of that year, [the *Mayflower*] was ordered equipped for war and sent to avenge the sinking of the *Maine*," wrote Lee Ping Quan's biographer Jim Miller. The *Mayflower* was recommissioned in 1905 as a presidential yacht. "Serving as the President's yacht," wrote Miller, "the *Mayflower*'s duties—of which carrying the Chief Executive on pleasure cruises was but incidental—were varied and colorful during her long period of service. She was an honorable veteran of wars; had helped in the protection of our naval interests in foraging seas; had served as flagship, and had been called upon to act as an envoy of good will, carrying important personages on diplomatic and social cruises."[6] As this ship's history illustrates, the *Mayflower* did not conform to what one normally visualizes when hearing the word "yacht," as on episodes of the television reality shows *Lifestyles of the Rich and Famous* or *Below Deck*. Instead, these ships were made to serve and protect the president.

For the yachts that came into presidential service, how did it happen that Asians were welcomed aboard, especially considering that most were not U.S. citizens? Since the 1860s, African Americans had dominated the navy's culinary and servant positions. They were known as "landsman," a term reclassified to "messmen" in 1893. Then, just before the end of the century, naval officers shifted toward a marked preference for Asian servants, especially the Chinese. After the Spanish-American War of 1898 and the cession of the Philippines from Spain to the United States, the U.S. Navy expanded recruitment to all parts of Asia, but particularly the Philippines. According to the U.S. Navy website, "President William McKinley signed an executive order in 1901 allowing the navy to enlist 500 Filipinos as part of the insular force. Secretary of the Navy John D. Long signed General Order No. 40, 8 April 1901, promulgating the executive order."[7]

Filipinos typically worked alongside Chinese and Japanese personnel below deck on navy ships, and that was certainly the case on the *Dolphin* and the *Mayflower*. In fact, during the peace talks, Roosevelt quartered the Japanese delegation on the *Dolphin* because so many of its sailors were Japanese nationals.[8] The Asian seamen listed (by position) as serving in the mess department at this time were Chinoski Masak (title illegible), Hsaio Makino (cabin steward), Cho Masaki (cabin cook), Fukusa Oka (mess attendant, third class), Kisogee Sato (cabin steward), Yukichi Yesaki (wardroom cook), and Jutaro Yawada (steward cook).[9]

Before the talks began, the president greeted the parties at his summer home in Oyster Bay, New York, on August 6, 1905. From there, the delegations sailed to Portsmouth, New Hampshire. Despite the favorable conditions, achieving peace was not inevitable. Tensions between the delegations were thick enough to cut with a butter knife and egos were as inflated and fragile as a soufflé. Knowing this, Roosevelt set an amicable tone by delicately choreographing the first meal served on his presidential yacht, the *Mayflower*, while still in Oyster Bay. According to a contemporary account:

> *Careful to avoid any strain, President Roosevelt as soon as possible after the introductions suggested that the party proceed to the main saloon, where luncheon was waiting. The president himself led the party, followed in order by M. Witte, Baron Komura, Ambassador Rosen,*

The USS Mayflower, *c. 1911.*

and Minister Takahira. Even the formation of this little procession involved a delicate diplomatic problem, but it was agreed that the president solved it admirably. Although the luncheon was a standing up affair, the president escorted the four envoys to chairs in one corner of the saloon, and in half a minute through tact and delicacy the whole party was engaged in animated conversation over the dishes.[10]

Roosevelt knew that something as trivial as where people sat in relation to him could be interpreted as a sign of disrespect that would dissolve the entire effort, and he was determined that the peace talks would not be derailed before they even started.

AH LOY

Enter Ah Loy, the *Mayflower*'s chief cook, who orchestrated a different kind of harmony for President Roosevelt in the ship's galley below deck. Loy, a Chinese national who was several months into his naval assignment, was responsible for the remarkable and possibly peace-saving meal. What was served for that luncheon is not known, but we have an inkling of how the chef felt that day from a newspaper interview published years later. In the article, Loy admitted he "was a bit frightened" by the entire situation, but obviously things went swimmingly—especially for his boss, President Roosevelt.[11]

What we do know is that Loy supervised a culinary team, known as the messmen's branch of the ship, ranging between fifteen to twenty stewards, cooks, bakers, and mess attendants. We also know that during the peace negotiations, Asian messmen dominated the *Mayflower*'s galley kitchen. Some of Loy's crewmates (by position) were Ah Chung (wardroom cook), Chew Chung (steward cabin cook), Hoo Gaui (steerage steward), Ah Hu (mess attendant first class), Haw Hui (mess attendant first class), Fong Liu (steward), Ah Lung (mess attendant), Chiu Way (mess attendant), Ah Wing (mess attendant), Ah Wong (cabin cook), and Hung Ying (cabin cook).[12] Several shared the first name "Ah," which, according to a Chinese author of a book about Chinese restaurants, is "a colloquial Chinese prefix used with a shortened form of someone's name, usually one-syllable to express familiarity."[13] Previously, during William McKinley's presidency, other Asian recruits served on the *Mayflower*. The yacht's June 23, 1900, muster roll lists Shiba Fukuhara (wardroom steward), Ah Hee (mess attendant), Sorzavola Ono (cabin steward), Tsukasa Okida (cabin steward), and Yoji Row (commander in chief's cook). In later years, newspaper articles mentioned Ing Yee Yue and Masa Watanabe as presidential yacht cooks during this era.[14] These individuals are some of the earliest documented Asian heritage culinary professionals who served in presidential

The USS Dolphin, *c. 1910.*

food service, and their culinary legacy stretches to the present day.

History gives only a small taste of the meals that Loy cooked on the *Mayflower*. Yet one surviving relic of that era is a handwritten luncheon menu on stationery with a sketch of the *Mayflower*, dated July 21, 1905. The following items were served for a midday feast that Loy supervised: clam chowder, crackers, radishes, pickles, broiled spring chicken on toast, shoofly potatoes, cantaloupes, and coffee.[15] It is no surprise that Loy's culinary talent impressed the delegates and got the talks off to a good start. Ultimately the delegations reached a peace agreement, and President Roosevelt received the 1906 Nobel Peace Prize for his mediation.

U.S. Navy recruitment of Asian men continued at an accelerated pace, and the dramatic efforts to enlist them played out in muster rolls—official lists of a ship's personnel—including the *Mayflower*. Every quarter, the *Mayflower*'s captain had to complete a summary of "Discharges, Desertions, Deaths, and Citizenship." The category Citizenship was broken down into these subcategories: Citizens (native born); Naturalized Citizens; Declared Intentions to Become Citizens; Aliens, Resident in the United States; Aliens, Nonresident; Apprentices (native born); and Apprentices (foreign born). Over the next couple of decades, the Asian presence grew so much that subsequent *Mayflower* captains created separate ship log categories for Chammorro (from the Mariana Islands), Filipino, Hawaiian, Japanese, Philippine island [*sic*], P.I., Residents of the Philippine Islands, and Samoan seamen, as well as Puerto Rican seamen. At the same time, as naval historian Frederick S. Harrod observed, the number of African Americans serving on naval ships plummeted. "The number of Filipinos rose rapidly and by 1914 had surpassed the number of blacks. . . . As blacks retired or left the service, their numbers declined, reaching a low of 441 in 1932—0.55% of the total enlisted force," Harrod wrote.[16] By the time of the Coolidge presidency, only white and Asian seamen served on the presidential yacht.

Despite an increasing presence, Asian heritage cooks rarely made dishes from their own countries for a ship's crew. The 1920 edition of the *U.S. Navy Cook-Book* did not contain a single recipe from an Asian cuisine.[17] As mentioned above, Loy made a luncheon in July 1905 that featured clam chowder. Another documented example of a special meal that Loy prepared occurred when U.S. Navy Secretary Charles Joseph Bonaparte, a distant relative of Napoleon Bonaparte, and his wife hosted President Roosevelt and First Lady Edith Roosevelt in 1906. Being a proud Marylander, Secretary Bonaparte served a meal featuring Chesapeake Bay specialties such as "terrapin, canvas back duck, [and] fried chicken." The beverages included "the usual wines" and punch "ladled from the handsome bowl from which Ambassador Rosen, on behalf of the Russian mission at Portsmouth presented recently to the officers of the *Mayflower*," reported a newspaper.[18] Once

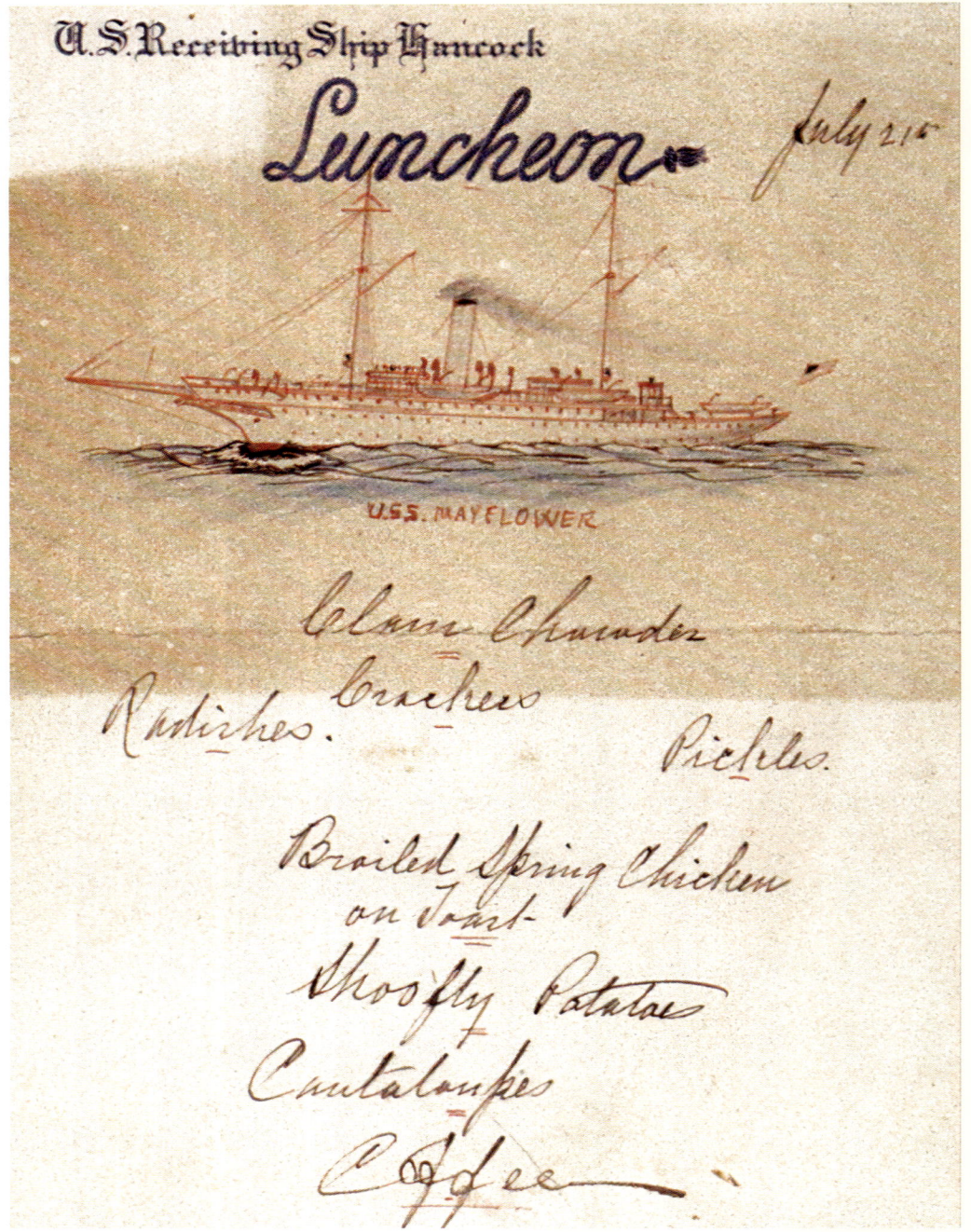

A handwritten menu for a luncheon overseen by Chef Ah Loy on the USS Mayflower. *Clam chowder, broiled spring chicken, shoofly potatoes, and cantaloupes are listed.*

again, history comes full circle in a way. Not until 1927 had palates changed enough for the U.S. Navy cookbook to begin including dishes like "beef chop suey" (an American invention) and "curried mutton."[19]

Chef Ah Loy's newspaper interviews shed some light on his personal history and professional career. He recounted how he "came to America from China when he was 17 and worked as [a] cook for a private family in California until he joined the navy to 'see the world' in 1900." Five years later, he became the *Mayflower*'s first presidential cook while serving Theodore Roosevelt. Loy's only comment about President Roosevelt was that "he's a heavy sleeper" because he slept through an accident that the yacht had with a lumber schooner while cruising to New London, Connecticut.[20] Loy had much more to say about the Roosevelt children, and it was all joy. "'My most pleasant memories of all were of the Roosevelt children,' said Ah Loy. He told how they jumped first to the galley, where they knew 'some goodies' awaited them."[21]

After Roosevelt's presidency, Loy continued to serve

aboard the *Mayflower*, and when it came to what others liked, and disliked, eating, Chef Loy noted that President Woodrow Wilson loved frog legs but dished more about Warren G. Harding. "Very quiet, but very nice," Loy said. "He liked broiled lobster. And every trip Mrs. Coolidge ordered chop suey—every trip." President Harding seems to be the only one to truly show his appreciation for Loy. "One day on a trip," Loy recalled to a reporter, "the steward told Loy that the President wished to see him. Wiping his flour covered hands on his apron, Loy hurried upstairs and went into the dining room. President Harding, who was eating, put down his fork, and standing up, shook hands with the little chef, and told him that he appreciated his good work. Mrs. Harding, too, was very kind to Loy, and when she had visitors aboard, she always took them to inspect the kitchen."[22] Chef Loy also noted some of the standard fare. "Before a trip," Ah Loy said, "the assistant chef always prepared a large batch of almond cakes, referred to by the crew as 'economy cookies' because they [were not] larger than a 25-cent coin."[23]

Chef Loy was dismissed in mid-June 1929. According to a newspaper report of the time, it is not "that Mr. Hoover is dissatisfied with his work, but having no inclination for yachting, the Chief Executive has ordered the *Mayflower* decommissioned." With that decision, both Chef Loy and the USS *Mayflower* fulfilled the article's title, "Out of a Job."[24] It seems fitting that Loy and the *Mayflower* both served the presidency for the exact same amount of time. Loy admitted that he had not accumulated any life savings. Though he retired receiving two-thirds of his regular pay, Loy fully intended to seek employment with a private family after his naval retirement.[25] Unfortunately, further details of Chef Loy's life and death postretirement are unknown.

Upon his retirement, Chef Ah Loy says good-bye to a fellow crew member on the USS Mayflower, *1929.*

SHIRO TSURUSAKI

Shiro Tsurusaki, who served as the *Mayflower*'s chief steward for several years, is another well-documented Asian heritage presidential chef from this era. As chief steward, Tsurusaki would have been in charge of managing the staff, procuring food, developing menus, supervising the cooking, and preparing meals. Tsurusaki's life of adventure began well before his service on the *Mayflower*. Sometime in the 1870s, according to a newspaper article, he "was born at sea on a British ship." Not much is known about his childhood and early adulthood, but he eventually served on a late nineteenth-century British expedition to Patagonia in South America. On the trip, he received a most unfortunate souvenir: a large snake bite that permanently scarred his back.[26] Yet Tsurusaki enjoyed a sixteen-year naval career, and he reportedly "cruised 200,000 miles on the presidential yacht, including trips to Panama, Cuba, Mexican ports, and all along the Atlantic coast."[27]

Newspaper reports also give us glimpses of Tsurusaki's personal life. On June 29, 1907, while living in Brooklyn and aged 30, Tsurusaki married a woman named Margaritta.[28] Newspaper reports varied the spelling of her first name as Marguerite and her last name as Sigand and Sigando and her nationality as French or Italian.[29] They had two children: Josephine born in 1908 and Eugene born in 1909. By 1918, Tsurusaki's marriage made news, but for the wrong reasons. Tsurusaki filed for divorce, alleging that his wife had an affair with a Filipino national named Ambrucio Palustra.[30] Tsurusaki married again in 1921, to Lillie Carey, a divorcée.[31]

In June 1922, Tsurusaki was appointed the first steward of the newly formed Congressional Country Club in Maryland. A newspaper report of the time said that he owed his appointment to "the influence of Lieutenant Colonel C. O. Sherrill, military aide to the president, and Rear Admiral Cary T. Grayson, [both] members of the board of governors of the club." Tsurusaki worked there in his spare time until he officially retired in November 1922, after sixteen years of naval service.[32]

During his career, Tsurusaki got mixed signals about whether he would be socially accepted in the United States. The navy certainly welcomed him as a seaman, but Americans in general were showing increasing hostility, mainly because of a perceived threat from Japanese immigration. "Between 1901 and 1908, a time of unrestricted immigration," reported a commission, "127,000 Japanese entered the U.S."[33] The numbers of new arrivals peaked in 1907 with as many as 30,000 Japanese immigrants counted (economic and living conditions were particularly bad in Japan at this point as a result of the Russo-Japanese War).[34]

For this reason, Tsurusaki inadvertently made national headlines again in 1922. Previously, on December 18, 1918, he had become a naturalized U.S. citizen thanks to the Alien Naturalization Act of 1918, which granted aliens citizenship if they served in World War I. Tsurusaki's successful citizenship application was later heavily criticized by some because he had not seen any actual combat. Yet the controversy did not prevent him from being a citizen. Emboldened by his newly minted citizenship, in January 1921 Tsurusaki went to court to have his name legally changed from "Tsurusaki Shiro," as he had incorrectly been called for years, to his birth name, "Shiro Tsurusaki."[35] Any good feelings that Tsurusaki had about his adopted country were likely muted when the U.S. Supreme Court ruled in *Takao Ozawa v. United States* that Japanese nationals could not apply for citizenship under the Naturalization Act of 1906 since they did not meet the legal definition of being "white."[36] As a result of the court's decision, Tsurusaki's citizenship, despite years of loyal presidential service, was immediately revoked.[37] The anti-Japanese sentiment continued to rise and crested when Congress passed the Immigration Act of 1924, which effectively ended legal Japanese immigration. By 1930, even the navy fully stopped enlisting Asian men.[38]

Despite the lack of social acceptance, Tsurusaki accepted the navy's call to serve his adopted country once again. President Warren Harding personally requested that Tsurusaki come out of retirement and serve as his chief steward on a special trip aboard the transport ship USS *Henderson*.[39] Harding hoped that this "Voyage of Understanding," with stops in Alaska and along the West Coast, would help his sagging popularity as he geared up for a presidential reelection campaign. Harding's doctor thought the trip would do him good and relieve stress. The "voyage" began in June 1923 with a cross-country railroad trip to San Francisco. From there, the presidential party boarded the *Henderson*, with Tsurusaki as chief steward, and headed north toward Alaska. The Alaska itinerary included Sitka, Juneau, Seward, Ketchikan, and Metlakatla.[40]

Health concerns emerged as the voyage turned south to return to the United States. As June Allen wrote in an

Chef Shiro Tsurusaki during his service as chief steward on the USS Mayflower, *1921.*

Chef Shiro Tsurusaki stands in front of the West Wing with the State, War and Navy Building behind him, c. 1922.

article reprinted online by the Alaska Historical Society:

> *The touring party members had been eating shellfish during the entire sea voyage, going and coming. But it was two days out of Sitka that the president first complained of sharp abdominal pains, but suffered no vomiting. Shellfish was suspected. But in hindsight no one could remember how the crabs had been delivered or by whom. And no one else became ill although many of the party had eaten crab.*
>
> *When the ship docked at Vancouver B.C., the president managed to address a crowd of some 40,000 well-wishers, but he was still feeling weak and ill. More problems were to arise. The following morning the* Henderson's *boiler room flooded and as all hands were called to action, the passengers too ran on deck just in time to see the big transport ram a smaller ship that sank in the fog. The president was said to have lost his good nature and was heard to say, "I hope this boat sinks." On departing after a stop in Seattle, the ill-fated* Henderson *rammed another vessel. It was not a pleasant voyage south! By the time the ship reached San Francisco, the president was seriously ill.*[41]

On August 1, 1923, the traveling party disembarked from the *Henderson* and the Hardings checked into the posh Palace Hotel while the president battled what was thought to be food poisoning. He died the next day.

After his naval service, Tsurusaki briefly operated a restaurant, appropriately called the Mayflower House, at Nihil Farm near Marlboro, Maryland (probably Upper Marlboro). During the summer of 1932, he ran various newspaper advertisements touting his experience as a former steward on a presidential yacht and cooking for six presidents (it was actually four).[42] To drive the point home, the advertisements prominently featured a sketch of the yacht just so that it would not be confused with the carrack that transported the Pilgrims in the early 1600s. Some advertisements promised diners "true Southern Hospitality," while others promised a taste of Asia by listing "curry rice" and "sukiyuki" [*sic*] as specialties.[43] Unfortunately, the restaurant was short-lived, and Tsurusaki returned to full retirement.

On a chilly December day in 1934, Tsurusaki went to Bolling Air Force Base on the eastern banks of the Potomac River near Washington, D.C. The occasion was an air show to commemorate the thirty-first anniversary of Orville and Wilbur Wright's successful first flight at Kitty Hawk, North Carolina. Tsurusaki caught a cold and went to bed on Christmas Day. He developed pneumonia and died on December 29 at the Naval Hospital in Washington, D.C.[44]

Chef Tsurusaki touted his experience cooking for six presidents when advertising the opening of his restaurant in 1932.

Even though the U.S. Navy no longer recruited new Asian heritage messmen in the early 1930s, those already in the navy's ranks continued to serve with distinction. By that time, Filipinos dominated the navy's culinary operations. Their stories of life aboard the presidential yachts are usually lost to recorded history and live on primarily in family stories passed down to their descendants. A notable exception is a remarkable individual who took the time to make sure that his story was told and provided the most detailed biography of a presidential cook up to that point. That man is Lee Ping Quan, and what follows in the next chapter is a distilled version of his memoir cookbook, *To a President's Taste*.

CHAPTER TWO

IN DEPTH WITH LEE PING QUAN

It is not good to be without a cook, but it is very much worse to have a bad one.
—LEE PING QUAN

Lee Ping Quan, seen here in his naval uniform, served as a chef for Presidents Warren G. Harding and Calvin Coolidge on the USS Mayflower *from 1922 to 1929.*

In the late 1930s, a former presidential yacht chef named Lee Ping Quan sat down for multiple interviews recorded by a journalist named Jim Miller. The interviews formed the opening chapters of a memoir cookbook containing more than four hundred of Quan's recipes. What follows in this chapter is a condensed version of his biographical sketch from the cookbook, together with some additional material.

Lee Ping Quan was born in Lung Mon Village, "The Dragon Door Village," in China's Kwangtung Province. He grew up in Canton (today Guangzhou), China, sometime in the late 1880s. As a child, he walked down the street of the Seven Lotus Flowers and watched the ships at the city's public quays along the Chu-Kiang River (today Zhu Jiang, part of the Pearl River system), where workers unloaded a dizzying array of food products. Comprehending Quan's humble beginnings, biographer Jim Miller mused: "Who, for example, could have foretold that this little Chinese boy was to stamp the dust of quaint old Canton from his tiny sandals, turn his face westward and become, at last, the chief steward, personal chef and honored friend of two presidents in our own United States!"[1]

Quan could not have had a better culinary mentor than his uncle, Li Wan Sun—a culinary legend in his own right. Sun was a renowned chef, cookbook author, and restaurateur. He owned a Canton tea house that was "patronized by all the dignitaries and notables of the city"[2] and the Pagoda House, a popular Hong Kong inn. Sun was also a notable figure in the Canton Restaurant Guild, and he prepared many incomparable State Dinners for China's political elite.

Quan's eventful boyhood differed greatly from that of the average Chinese youth. He began his apprenticeship under Sun at a very young age. When he was five years old, his family moved to the Philippine Islands, where Sun was now the chief cook at the Manila Hotel. Then, by the age of eight, Quan had begun a decade-long education at a Manila cooking school while simultaneously working hard to improve his English. At age 20, he enlisted in the U.S. Navy, and during World War I he served as the officer's steward on the USS *Barry*, whose missions took him as far as the Mediterranean Sea.[3]

President Warren G. Harding boards the USS Mayflower, *April 27, 1922.*

President Calvin Coolidge enjoys a voyage on the USS Mayflower, *April 1925.*

After marrying in 1904 and having a son, Quan relocated his family to China to fulfill his wife's desire to immerse their son in "true Chinese customs."[4] While there, he followed his uncle's footsteps and prepared meals for the Canton Restaurant Guild. Despite such culinary adventures and a comfortable life, Quan wanted to return to naval service, so he reenlisted and served on several U.S. destroyers and torpedo boats. Quan's fame as a chef spread all over the navy, and during President Warren G. Harding's presidency, in 1922, while on the USS *Laub* in San Diego, California, he was assigned to serve as the steward and chef on the presidential yacht, the *Mayflower*. In this role, Quan cooked exclusively for the first family and their guests. He later reminisced about his early impressions of the *Mayflower*:

> *Forward on the main deck, beyond the dining and reception rooms, was the President's galley, fitted with two oil-burning regulation Navy ranges, and various other kitchen equipment, all immaculately sparkling and spotlessly clean. There were two other galleys on the ship—the officer's galley and the galley for the crew's mess....*
>
> *The chinaware was the ordinary regulation Navy crockery of the variety used in the officer's mess. It was different only in the fact that it had for a decoration a narrow gold band and the official crest. Substantial usefulness was the chief characteristic of the equipment on board.*
>
> *The* Mayflower *was no more a personal luxury to the President than were his aides or the members of his cabinet. She was often used to give him some sorely needed relaxation or an opportunity to puzzle out some gnarled problems of state away from the interruptions of his executive offices.*[5]

Whenever the first families he served decided to "get away from it all," Quan was there to ensure their comfort.

Quan was already somewhat of a celebrity chef in navy circles by the time he joined the *Mayflower*, and during his tenure he added presidents (Harding and Calvin Coolidge), first ladies, military leaders, foreign royalty, and diplomats to his informal fan club. Menus, including those from various diplomatic and presidential cabinet dinners, were among his most treasured mementos. Quan fondly recalled a diplomatic dinner that President Coolidge hosted on November 8, 1925, for the Japanese delegation of Prince Yasuhiko Asaka, Princess Nobuko Asaka, and the Japanese ambassador to the United States, Tsuneo Matsudaira.[6] Some believed that "the ancient animosity between the Chinese and the people of Nippon was almost healed by a masterly feast prepared by Quan—In fact, it was one of his supreme efforts."[7] As another act of culinary diplomacy, World War I hero General John J. Pershing was so impressed by one of Quan's meals that he remarked, "If such delicious food had been served to our dough-boys we would have won the War long ago." Quan replied, "Thank you very much for your compliment, sir, I have served as chef on several different destroyers and torpedo boats, and the officers often said to me that food had a lot to do with winning the war."[8]

Perhaps Quan's fame reached an apex in the mid-1920s. As Miller noted, "It was around this time that the U.S. Navy Department asked Quan to assume the lead in a moving picture with a turkey acting in the chief supporting role." The crew of a cameraman and six sailors captured what we would now call a "turkey farm-to-table" experience. The film begins with Quan capturing a live turkey, then progresses with him prepping the turkey in the White House Kitchen, and ends as "the turkey made its exit from the stove, a beautiful, golden-brown in hue, ready to be carved and served for the Thanksgiving feast."[9]

Akin to other presidential chefs, Quan's skill set often required problem solving. On one particular night, First Lady Florence Harding requested ten dozen lobsters for dinner. As told to the biographer:

> Quan scoured the markets but was able to find but two lonesome ones. Upon returning to the ship with only two lobsters, he told Mrs. Harding that he was unable to find any more. Greatly disappointed, she commissioned fifteen officers to corner the sea food market and fetch back enough lobsters to serve her guests. They were even more unfortunate than Quan had been, for after fine-combing the highways and byways they returned empty-handed—there were no lobsters to be had. Quan, in the meantime, resorted to strategy; he cached the two lobsters until after the dinner was over and the company had left, then he served them to the President and Mrs. Harding for a midnight supper.[10]

Stories like this highlight Quan's talent for constantly innovating. Quan had not only mastered the American style of cooking but also excelled in preparing cuisines from almost any country in the world. Always, when aboard ship, he would go ashore at every port and browse around different eating places to learn some new dish. Then he would serve it to the wardroom or the captain after everybody had forgotten about the port where he learned it.

Sensing the American public's appetite to know more about presidential palates, Quan described the favorite foods of the families that he served. President Harding started his day by having liver, bacon, French fried potatoes, waffles, syrup, and coffee in the mahogany and blue dining room of the *Mayflower*. For Mrs. Harding, it was oatmeal and cream. If President Harding wanted a lighter breakfast option, he would have cornflakes. Other favorites were roast squab with currant jelly and strawberries. "But the daintiest and most toothsome morsels in the president's eyes," wrote Miller, "were Quan's almond cookies, originated by the expert cook himself. Almond cookies worthy to go down in history with the famous tartlets of Rageneau in Rostand's *Cyrano*."[11] Dinner for the Hardings was formal. On these occasions, the presidential mahogany table was artistically decorated with blue candles set tastefully on a blue tablecloth, with baskets of blue flowers arranged at attractive angles. The service was of solid silver. The menu usually consisted of roasted almonds, olives, homemade candy, appetizers, grapefruit cocktail, green turtle soup, fish à la king, sweet potato croquettes, creamed cauliflower, spinach rolls stuffed with avocado, salad with cheese straws, rainbow jello in an orange basket with whipped cream, almond cookies, coconut pie, demitasse, cigars and cigarettes, and white rock candy.[12]

Quan loved the Coolidges. They extensively used the yacht, "taking his family and a few friends down the

Chef Lee Ping Quan makes one of President Coolidge's favorite dishes, eggs stuffed with caviar, onboard the USS Mayflower.

Potomac whenever he could snatch a little time from the press of business in Washington." Quan also added that First Lady Grace Coolidge "was the perfect first lady of the land." For breakfast, President Coolidge enjoyed pork sausage and waffles, "with a special maple syrup sent him from Vermont in five-gallon tins." Mrs. Coolidge preferred codfish balls for breakfast. For other meals, the president fancied quail, curried veal with condiments, and caviar in egg on toast. Quan emphasized, "But still . . . I'm sure President Coolidge preferred my jelly roll best. He had a very sweet tooth. I believe that desserts should be an important item in the service at a grand feast."[13]

Dinners aboard the *Mayflower* when the Coolidges entertained were elaborate and called for all the skill at Quan's command. Four assistant cooks and eight table stewards were employed to prepare and serve for the banquets and numerous courses of the dinners. The band from the naval station at Washington would play on deck or, if the weather was bad, in the library, which was not far from the dining saloon.

Much more fun than the formal dinners, to Quan, were the comparatively simple lunches and teas that he used to serve the Coolidge family on the decks of the yacht during the long, lazy afternoons on the Potomac. Although most of Quan's duties were confined to the *Mayflower*, he made daily visits to the White House, where he prepared countless tidy dishes with his own hands. In recognition of this special service, he saved many valuable and treasured letters from the late Warren Harding, Calvin Coolidge, Mrs. Coolidge, and the younger Coolidges.

Before retiring to private life, Mrs. Coolidge asked Quan to teach her how to make chop suey "in the real

Canton fashion" rather than what one typically found in the Chinese American restaurants of that era. Never mind that chop suey is a purely American invention. She enthusiastically wrote: "Dear Quan: Many thanks for the delicious chop suey. My friends and I have eaten chop suey in many places, but never found any as good as yours. Sometime I hope you will teach me to make it. Sincerely yours, Grace Coolidge."[14] In addition to being delicious, and a favorite dish of his wife's, one food writer speculated that President Coolidge also loved the dish because "he was one of our most frugal presidents, and this dish makes a pound and a half of chicken go a long way!"[15]

In 1929 Herbert Hoover began his presidency, the USS *Mayflower* began its thirty-first year of naval service, and Quan became eligible to retire from the navy. It was rumored that President Hoover was to put the famous yacht out of commission during his term, and when he did, Quan retired. In some circles, much like his predecessor Ah Loy, Quan had personified the *Mayflower*.

After his retirement, Quan gained a reputation for cake making, and he sent one annually to the Coolidges as well as to others. He told his biographer that "he would go through the most intensive and exhausting methods of packing these gifts safely to insure their safe arrival. Besides, he would have the express company describe to him minutely the way the cake would be transported, the time of its pulling in to each station enroute, and had them guarantee its delivery at the Coolidge home in plenty of time for an early dinner."[16] A thank-you note was the only reciprocation needed, and it always brought him joy.

Yet Quan did not share his cake joy and generosity with everyone. Knowing about the numerous cakes that the Coolidges enjoyed, a reporter had the following exchange with Quan:

"You have made so many birthday cakes for the Coolidges, are you ever going to make one for President Hoover?"

Quickly Quan replied, "No, sir, no cake for President Hoover."

"What! No cake for President Hoover!" the reporter teased.

"Most emphatically, No! President Hoover put the Mayflower *out of service."*

"Oh," questioned the reporter, "just because he put the Mayflower *out of commission he doesn't get any cake?"*

Quan's quaint retort was: "No Mayflower—*no cake."*[17]

As one can see, "salty" best describes the flavor profile of Quan's feelings toward President Hoover.

The *Mayflower*'s final act ushered in Quan's next act as a restaurateur. In early April 1929, urged by several of his friends among the high officers of the navy, he opened a restaurant at 28 West Fifty-First Street in New York City.[18] The restaurant's menu featured the food he served on the *Mayflower*, and his core customer base was from his network of navy and presidential contacts. Opened during Prohibition, the restaurant was also alcohol free. This venture was made possible by the investment of Helen de Bogart de Rochemont. She heard about Quan from her brother-in-law, Louis de Rochemont, who made movies for the navy. Given her own desire to get involved in the hospitality industry and knowing that Quan was looking for something to do in his sudden retirement, Rochemont sold him on the restaurant idea.[19] Quan and Rochemont were also buoyed when the navy announced the restaurant's opening in its *Bureau of Navigation Bulletin*.[20] To emphasize Quan's presidential connection, Rochemont designed the restaurant's interior to evoke being aboard a yacht's deck. As Miller shared:

The influence of his love for the sea could easily be traced in the decorations of his restaurant. In fact, it was very suggestive of the famous yacht where he had so many of his culinary triumphs.

The walls were broken by port-holes, resplendent in glistening brass and glowing with yellow lights set back of them. The main dining room was long, and narrow, shaped like a yacht and painted a dead white, with the plump circle of a life-preserver hanging inside a front window.

One side of the room was open to the sea!

The diners on that side sat under the very crest of tall blue-green waves whose foamy tops seemed about to engulf the tables. In the far distance a three-stack steamer belched ribbons of black smoke. The tables, with their straight-backed rattan chairs, were cozy, and seemed to call for the presence of those snowy-garbed celestials who appeared to glide softly bearing trays of food

Lee Ping Quan in the New York City restaurant he opened in 1929, designed to resemble the interior of the USS Mayflower.

and drink. Overhead was stretched an orange awning with blue-green stripes, through which light filtered giving a sunny, out-doors effect combined with coolness and tranquility.[21]

One food writer described Quan's restaurant as "truly a restful spot in seething New York, with the effect of a deck restaurant at sea, minus the *mal de mer* [seasickness]."[22]

Despite the glitz and extensive support from naval and presidential patrons, Quan's endeavor encountered troubled waters on opening night. The soup was not hot, the service slow, and the table settings not right. Quan was frustrated by employees ("handpicked," said Quan, after consultation with Chinese fathers and uncles),[23] who did not share his passion for hospitality and excellent service. Even though he had given them stern pep talks, they had failed to measure up. Things changed when a despondent Quan was rescued in a way by a president he faithfully served. After a tiring, discouraging, sleepless night, he returned to the restaurant to check the mail.

Suddenly his heart started thumping madly. There in his hand was a large envelope of a fine texture. His name and address were inscribed on it in a firm and clear hand—and the postmark was Northampton, Mass. Quan opened it rapidly and carefully—even though his fingers shivered—and read in the same firm script:

"My dear Quan: Mrs. Coolidge and I wish you every success with your restaurant. We shall always remember how kind you were to us when you were on the U.S.S. Mayflower, *and how well you fed us. Yours, Calvin Coolidge."*[24]

Quan cried with gratitude that President Coolidge took the time to encourage him. He also huddled up his staff when they reported for work, "gave them a scathing lecture on their shortcomings of the night before," showed them Coolidge's letter, and translated it into Cantonese in order to motivate them. Quan said that

IN DEPTH WITH LEE PING QUAN

afterward, "Each one worked as though he were six men. They finally understood and they never forgot. They all gave me splendid service until I retired from the restaurant business some years later."²⁵

Nonetheless, the New York restaurant did not last long. Quan was disappointed that, despite their encouragement, the Coolidges never patronized his establishment during the multiple trips they made to New York. In addition to the joy he would have gotten from feeding his favorite first family, perhaps Quan thought that their visit would generate some much-needed buzz. Alas, the economic headwinds ended up being too strong for the sailor-chef-cum-restaurateur. By mid-December 1929, a month and a half after the stock market crash that ushered in the Great Depression, Quan declared bankruptcy and closed his restaurant.²⁶ The following year, when about one-third of Manhattan restaurants "went under," Quan had a stint helming the kitchen at a Broadway nightclub.²⁷

Quan left New York City in 1932 to give the restaurant business another try in two unlikely spots located in Maine: Lincoln, a logging and paper-milling town in the central part of the state, and Rockport, a community on the Atlantic Coast, just north of Portland.²⁸ In each locale, Quan replicated the menu and decor of his New York restaurant to attract summer tourists, and he heavily advertised in Maine newspapers as far north as Bangor, touting his *Mayflower* experience. Quan once promised, "Tasty Chinese and American dishes will be served in a manner that will be a treat you'll long remember."²⁹ Unfortunately, as the *Atlanta Constitution* reported, "People just didn't seem to want to eat like presidents in those lean years [of the Great Depression], and restaurant after restaurant closed behind Quan."³⁰

Curiously, Quan briefly mentioned his family early in his memoir, but never again. Quan's family remains invisible in the subsequent, and extensive, press coverage of him. By the time Miller interviewed him in 1938, Quan was a retiree living alone on a U.S. government pension in "a snug little apartment in the lower part of New York City."³¹ During this time, Quan declined numerous attempts to bring him out of retirement. Quan, with deep confidence in his own value, would not even consider a job unless it limited his workday to four hours and paid him at least $300 a month (a little more than $6,700 U.S. dollars in 2025).³² Quan did not have any takers, which was just fine with him since he could live well on his $75 a month navy pension. As Quan told a newspaper

Quan widely advertised his restaurants in Maine, identifying himself as the former chef of the USS Mayflower.

journalist, "The government supports me. . . . I have fun like hell."³³

Quan's biographer often interviewed Quan in his apartment. During one visit, Miller described a sumptuous meal Quan laid out for him:

> *It was fit for a king; and as we later learned, had been partaken of by many a king. There were appetizers of stuffed eggs, vari-colored and molded into shapes of flowers and leaves. There was a dish of rice and curry—the same dish that was President Coolidge's favorite—with the wealth of accompanying condiments. There were cookies of various kinds, salads—cool, delicious salads, composed of strange but tasty vegetables. There was a luscious dessert of a jello-stuffed, rainbow-hued orange; then came a strawberry short-cake, so beautifully decorated that we felt guilty to mar its elegance by cutting it. Besides, small, colored plates stood around everywhere, loaded with artistically prepared Chinese candies, jellied fruits and assorted nuts.*³⁴

Even late in his life, Quan never lost his touch for hospitality and culinary excellence.

Quan was also quick to share the culinary wisdom he had accumulated over several decades from ports around the world. He urged beginning cooks to study and read cookbooks and maintain a standard of excellence. He was known to offer a benediction that would serve cooks well in contemporary times: "Neither is a meal a matter of expense alone, nor an obligation of a social debt. A good meal is a combination of the right guests, fitness of things, temperature, variety and time. The mere question of satisfying one's hunger is simple. We can walk along nibbling bread and stop at a well for water. However, dinner today, in our complicated existence, is a matter of interest which should always be paramount in social life."[35]

Then came the Japanese attack on Pearl Harbor. Quan immediately contacted Admiral Chester W. Nimitz, who had been a young ensign on the torpedo boat *Decatur* where Quan served as a steward in 1908.[36] Quan wanted to reenlist. He found out that the Japanese had bombed and destroyed two of his homes in Canton, China.[37] By then, Quan was in his early 60s, and his request was denied due to his age. Yet he had demonstrated that he still had some fire in him. He died in 1943.[38]

While the stories of Loy, Quan, and Tsurusaki are closely tied to the *Mayflower*, other boats pressed into presidential yacht service were also staffed with Asian cooks, although maybe less notable than these three chefs. Former White House correspondent Kenneth T. Walsh observed that President Franklin D. Roosevelt "started his presidency by taking pleasure trips on the 104-foot *Sequoia* but eventually began using the USS *Potomac*, a 165-foot former Coast Guard cutter with an elevator that could carry the wheelchair-bound president between decks."[39] Roosevelt used the *Potomac* for a mix of business and pleasure. He fished nearly every weekend from May until November where the Potomac River emptied into the Chesapeake Bay. The crew joined him, and the cooks would prepare the day's catch on the spot. When they caught eels, "the Filipino cabin boys loved them."[40] The president often had some of his White House favorites show up on the yacht's menu. Jack Lynch, a white seaman who served on the presidential yacht in the 1930s, noted, "I recall that a favorite supper of President Roosevelt's when we'd be returning on a Sunday night was scrambled eggs and little link sausages. When he had that, our cooks would prepare the same thing for the crew. We liked it, too."[41]

President Harry Truman, said Walsh, "hosted poker games aboard the *Sequoia* and the USS *Williamsburg*, a relatively fancy 242-foot yacht."[42] President Dwight D. Eisenhower was not really the yachting type, but President John F. Kennedy fully enjoyed being at sea. In addition to the *Sequoia*, Kennedy had the *Honey Fitz*, "an official presidential yacht that he renamed after his grandfather," wrote Walsh.[43] President Lyndon Baines Johnson occasionally used the *Sequoia* to lobby members of Congress, and President Richard Nixon used it extensively for work and play. President Gerald Ford, like Eisenhower, was not a seafarer, and he seldom used the yacht. The presidential yacht era came to a full stop when President Jimmy Carter, as part of a larger presidential austerity plan, auctioned off the *Sequoia* for a reported $286,000 in May 1977.[44] Public perception may also have been at issue.

In the early years, presidential yacht travel was not as controversial as it would be viewed today, as a form of recreation only elites could afford. In the first half of the twentieth century, Americans seemed to believe that presidents deserved a break from the stresses of the job, and yachting was just fine. Public opinion definitely shifted later in the century. Captain Giles M. Kelly, who wrote about the presidential yacht *Sequoia*, observed:

> *The term "yacht" has been a problem for* Sequoia *because some political figures, Presidents Jimmy Carter and Dwight D. Eisenhower among them, believed that close association with anything called a yacht while in office would tarnish their image because it might seem ostentatious. For that reason even today some congressional and administration leaders are reluctant to support her, let alone use her, though she is indeed a very modest yacht for the government of a superpower. At her inception, her designer referred to her not as a yacht, but as a "houseboat."*[45]

The prestige factor of the presidential yacht did cut both ways. Kelly related, "Years later, during his retirement, Gerald Ford was asked how he viewed *Sequoia*. '[She] was a superb yacht for special entertaining of presidential White House guests. The *Sequoia* was more informal than the White House itself, but significant as recognition of the prestige of the special guest. . . . I strongly believe [*Sequoia*] was a White House asset that could be used for constructive presidential entertainment.'"[46]

The waning of the presidential yacht era overlapped the advent of official presidential retreats on land, where Asian cooks continued to serve. One of the earliest and most long-lived witnesses to this transitional aspect of presidential history was a Filipino named Irineo Esperancilla. Like Quan, Esperancilla felt his story should be told. Ultimately, it would be, thanks to one of his tenacious granddaughters.

CHAPTER THREE

PRESIDENTIAL RETREATS AND THE WHITE HOUSE MESS

It is a great honor to be in the service of the president of the United States, but what a glorious thing it is to accomplish most of this service in the unique and unparalleled intimacy of a presidential yacht.
—IRINEO ESPERANCILLA

Irineo Esperancilla at work while serving as President Franklin D. Roosevelt's personal chef, 1938.

At countless family gatherings, elders often regale those assembled with tales of their exceptional ancestors. Irineo Esperancilla's family is no different. His granddaughter Melinda Dart recalls that when she was just three years old, her grandmother, Maryann, told her and other family members about her grandfather's service to several presidents, who called him "Issac" and "Chief" when they could not pronounce his name. Among many spectacular things, one thing stood out about Esperancilla. "My grandmother always talked about how he had already written a manuscript. It stayed in a trunk, and when she passed away, the trunk was given to me. So I knew that it was always my mission to get it published."[1]

Dart's quest was twofold. Her immediate passion was to complete her grandfather's mission to write his story, but she knew there was a broader calling at stake. "There's just a lot of things that people don't know about the Filipinos that served, especially during World War II, behind the scenes for the presidents. Right along during times of war, and times of peace, the Filipinos are behind the scenes holding down different things in the White House or at the retreats or yachts. People just don't know about that. So I really wanted to bring their stories to light."[2]

Years later, after going through Esperancilla's collection of letters, menus, and photos, in addition to the manuscript, Dart was ready to bring it all together. Yet the circumstances were challenging. With the COVID-19 pandemic in full swing, and a period of civil unrest, Dart completed and published *A Glimpse of Greatness: The Memoir of Irineo Esperancilla* in 2022. What follows, with Dart's permission, are some highlights from Esperancilla's incredible life story that bridges service at presidential retreats at sea and on land.

Growing up in the Philippines, from a young age Esperancilla felt "a calling to serve America."[3] On December 1, 1925, as a rising high school junior, he joined the U.S. Navy, first serving aboard the USS *Noa*. Then, after five years on the USS *Concord*, Esperancilla was assigned to serve the first family in an innovative way. President Herbert Hoover, having disposed of the *Mayflower*, nevertheless, like every president before him and since, still needed to "get away from it all" from time to time. Things often got hot for Hoover, due to pressures both from the job and from Mother Nature herself. He explained, "Washington's exhausting summer heat is known to several million people from acute experience. Eggs have been fried on the pavement."[4] Anyone who has experienced a summer in our nation's capital can relate. Camp Rapidan, the rustic new presidential retreat in the Blue Ridge Mountains, was a definite change from the upper-crust presidential getaways of the past. As Lawrence L. Knutson wrote in his definitive book *Away from the White House*, "There had never been anything quite like Hoover's fishing camp. Other presidents escaped Washington's summers at country homes or seaside cottages. Abraham Lincoln spent summers in a cottage at Washington's Soldiers' Home. Edith Roosevelt provided her husband a farmhouse near Charlottesville as an occasional refuge. But Rapidan Camp added a new dimension, evolving into something close to a private presidential resort and entertainment center."[5]

Knutson described the camp as situated where "the Rapidan meanders through Virginia's Madison County, below the spine of the Blue Ridge in a region that is now Shenandoah National Park, before flowing into the Rappahannock, which in turn empties into Chesapeake Bay. Oak, maple, hemlock, chestnut, and flowering laurel climb the hills and line the riverbanks."[6] Esperancilla described it as "an enchanting spot in the woods at the foot of the Blue Ridge Mountains. It's about one hundred miles west of Washington, D.C. There were several wooden houses under the shadow of beautiful trees between the Mill Prong and the Laurel Prong. These were brooks that joined the Rapidan River near the camp."[7] For Hoover, an avid angler, the opportunity to take advantage of Virginia's three-month-long mountain trout season was irresistible.[8]

While at the camp, Esperancilla spent most of his time in the dining hall, where meals were prepared and served, and at the steward's quarters in the northern part of the camp, near the Mill Prong.[9] In the spring of 1931, Esperancilla traveled with the Hoovers to Puerto Rico and the Virgin Islands aboard the USS *Arizona*. The Hoovers appreciated his service and gave him a special commendation before they left the White House.[10]

Camp Rapidan was operational for a limited time. When Franklin Roosevelt became president, the U.S. government created a top-secret and secure retreat in the Catoctin Mountains of Western Maryland, a few hours from Washington, D.C. Knutson noted, "Yielding to fancy, Roosevelt called it Shangri-La. He adopted the name from the popular 1933 James Hilton novel *Lost Horizon*. Its Shangri-La was a fictional sanctuary in the

I.

My name is Irineo...

I am Irineo Esperancilla, a retired Chief Steward ~~Mercy~~ of the United States Navy, I served in the Navy thirty years, from 1925 to 1955. I still wear a uniform which is that of a special guard's unit in a federal administration building in Washington, D.C. My colleagues always called me Ike because of my unpronounceable Spanish first name. I had to give up this nickname during my last t[wo ye]ars of continuous special service in the Navy, because Ike was also [ing] my last assignment. Another of my Bosse[s   ] Christian name either and called me [   ] who called me simply "chief". Howe[ver   ] the real chiefs because each of the [   ] Chief of the Armed Forces of the U[nited States   ]

The boss who called me Isaac was [   ] for the other Ike, he was Presid[ent   ] bosses, before and between them [   ] Harry S. Truman.

Between 1930 and 1955, I serve[d   ] a special steward attached to t[he   ] experience in my life but also [   ] States. I can summarize all my exp[erience   ] reaches

Irineo Esperancilla preserved the story of his presidential service with a typescript later adapted into book form by his granddaughter Melinda Dart.

Irineo Esperancilla offers President Franklin D. Roosevelt a cigarette on the Potomac *en route to a fishing trip in the Florida Keys, November 29, 1937.*

mountains of Tibet, isolated from the cares and alarms of an increasingly turbulent world. The government had less romantic names for FDR's retreat: Hi-Catoctin Camp No. 3 and Naval Support Facility."[11]

Esperancilla's service with Franklin and Eleanor Roosevelt was more varied than that with the Hoovers. He recounted in his memoir, "As Isaac, I served President Roosevelt on the USS *Sequoia* between 1933 and 1935; on the USS *Potomac* from 1936 to his death; in the White House; at Shangri-La; on the campaign train; on trips around the world; and very often at Hyde Park, his home above the Hudson River."[12] Esperancilla shared endearing episodes with Fala, FDR's beloved dog, lots of fun fish tales, scintillating dinners with dignitaries, and managing the egos of those same dignitaries.[13]

One of Esperancilla's most memorable encounters with a dignitary was with Soviet Premier Joseph Stalin at the Soviet Embassy in Tehran, Iran, in late fall 1943. FDR secretly met with British Prime Minister Winston Churchill and Stalin to strategize about winding down World War II to victory. What follows is an extended excerpt from Esperancilla's memoir of that occasion:

> *At the president's first meeting with Joseph Stalin, I served refreshments, cigars, and cigarettes. I immediately noted that Stalin did not take anything; he only puffed on his own pipe. During dinner later that day, I served all the guests as I normally did. As soon as I reached Stalin, he glanced suspiciously at me and signaled with his index finger that he did not want anything to eat. I could feel his piercing look as I served the other guests sitting*

around the long table. At first, I thought he did not like American food, or that he was not feeling well. I soon discovered that this was not the case. A bodyguard entered with a strange platter of foods I did not recognize and placed it before his boss. Stalin started to eat with a good appetite. I could not believe that a guest refused to eat the food offered by his host and brought his own meal! Although he was sitting at the top of history with the other great leaders of the free world, this man's wariness would not let him eat the food that all the other guests were enjoying.

Stalin continued to keep an eye on me that evening. I could not understand his words, but I finally heard him say to his interpreter, "Yapanets . . . Yapanets!" The uneasy Russian general spoke to my boss, saying, "I hope this man is not a Japanese." Stalin pointed directly at me. When the boss heard this, he laughed heartily and told the interpreter to inform Stalin that there was nothing to worry about. The president told the Soviet leader that I was a Filipino, son of an allied nation, and that I had worked for him for many years. Stalin seemed to be greatly relieved, and I was so glad the supreme leaders of the world could move on with their discussion of victory and a better future for suffering nations. I thought to myself, What kind of man could imagine that the president of the United States would bring an enemy with him when he met with other allied leaders? Stalin continued to have his own food served during our remaining time in Tehran; however, he did enjoy our assorted homemade cookies, made by the Filipinos. He gladly accepted them—even from me.[14]

Continuing his assigned duties despite Stalin's constant and intimidating glare, Esperancilla demonstrated his "grace under pressure."

Esperancilla served President Harry S. Truman on the USS *Augusta* as it sailed to Europe for the historic Potsdam Conference in 1945. Esperancilla's memoir did not mention any further trouble with Stalin. It was during his service on the USS *Williamsburg* that Esperancilla built a strong rapport with President Truman. He loved the way Truman interacted with everyone, even the lowest-ranked members of the crew, how he played the piano to relax while in his quarters, and his horrible luck playing cards. In November 1946, Esperancilla achieved another distinction by serving refreshments to President Truman 400 feet below the water's surface in a captured Nazi submarine, designated U-2513, that Truman was inspecting.[15] Esperancilla also served Truman at the Key West naval base known as "The Little White House" when he visited there for rest and relaxation.

When President Dwight D. Eisenhower decommissioned the USS *Williamsburg*, Esperancilla returned to Shangri-La, which Eisenhower renamed Camp David after his grandson. Thinking back on those days, Esperancilla recalled:

The highlight of the Camp David dinners was when President Eisenhower himself became the cook. By four thirty in the afternoon, the boss was already in our kitchen to direct and supervise the preparation of the tenderloin steak (which he would broil outside for his guests). He gave instructions to the chef to soak the meat in lots of melted butter and garlic salt. About forty-five minutes before dinner, it was my job to prepare and heat the charcoal on the outdoor grill. Then the president would come, tying a steward's apron around his waist, and place the meat on the grill. The boss would watch with the eyes of a real chef for a few seconds. He would tend to the steak, moving back and forth from the guests to the grill. The president also prepared the tasty sauce for the meat. The look on his face captured the joy he felt when the guests complimented him, asking for more of his famous tenderloin. I often thought photographers should be present to capture these proud and priceless moments of President Eisenhower cooking. I am a professional cook and have watched many of my great colleagues in the kitchen. In my opinion, President Eisenhower seemed to be a real master of the culinary art when he was behind the outdoor grill.[16]

This was only one example of President Eisenhower's cooking escapades. He is arguably the most avid cook to ever serve as president.

In July 1955, Esperancilla served President Eisenhower for the last time during a trip to Geneva, Switzerland. Later that month he retired from the U.S.

Chef Esperancilla delivers a newspaper to First Lady Mamie Eisenhower with her breakfast tray at Camp David.

Following his retirement from the navy, Esperancilla remained in touch with Presidents Truman, Eisenhower, and Hoover. In 1959, while working as a security guard at the Library of Congress, he crossed paths with Truman, who later signed a photograph of the encounter for his former steward.

Navy after thirty years serving four presidents. That was not his last presidential encounter, however. President Harry Truman recognized him during a 1959 visit to the Library of Congress where Esperancilla then worked as a guard. Truman sent him a note on May 14, 1959, to express his pleasure at once again seeing the trusted chief steward of the *Williamsburg*. Words cannot adequately express what Esperancilla meant to others, but Commander Edward L. Beach, U.S. Navy aide to the president of the United States, came close in a June 25, 1955, memorandum he sent to Esperancilla on the verge of his retirement: "I cannot but feel a deep sense of loss to this office, to the Navy, and to all of us aware of your faithful and almost legendary service to Presidents Hoover, Roosevelt, Truman and finally President Eisenhower. When all the histories for this era are written you may indeed have the gratification of reading between the lines and knowing to what extent you played an important part in the making of these histories."[17]

Later in his life, Esperancilla was diagnosed with colon cancer. According to Dart, he "made one last trip to the Philippines to see his family. He died in July 1976" and was laid to rest in Arlington National Cemetery.[18]

Subsequent presidents varied their use of Camp David. John Kennedy overwhelmingly preferred the family compound in Hyannis Port on the south shore of Cape Cod, Massachusetts, and Glen Ora, a leased 400-acre property in rural Virginia, near the town of Middleburg.[19] For Lyndon Johnson, his family ranch alongside the Pedernales River in central Texas's Hill Country was a favored place of refuge.[20] After a decade of neglect, Camp David was so deteriorated that the Richard Nixon administration ordered a major renovation. After that, President Nixon used it extensively.[21] President Gerald Ford made Camp David an open book by allowing press tours and his cabinet members to stay there with their families when the Fords were not using it. The Fords visited Camp David seventeen times, usually on weekends and once on Thanksgiving.[22] Under President Jimmy Carter, Camp David was best known for the historic peace negotiations between President Anwar Sadat of Egypt and Prime Minister Menachem Begin of Israel in September 1978.[23] President Reagan split his vacation time between Camp David and his California ranch.[24]

PRESIDENTIAL RETREATS AND THE WHITE HOUSE MESS

ARIEL DE GUZMAN

Then, with George H. W. Bush's presidency came an opportunity for another Asian heritage chef to cook at Camp David and other venues. Ariel De Guzman is the only Asian heritage chef besides Lee Ping Quan to create a memoir cookbook from his time in presidential food service—*The Bush Family Cookbook*.

Ariel De Guzman was born in Paniqui, Tarlac, which he described as "a quaint little town located seventy miles north of Manila, Philippines." De Guzman applied to join the U.S. Navy because "the people in my small hometown believed America was a land of opportunity and I, too, dreamed that a better life might be waiting for me in America. Those able to travel or relocate to the United States were considered very lucky." De Guzman felt he found fortune when his application was approved, and he was sworn in August 18, 1969, as a stewardsman. In that position, he cooked for a variety of military personnel. Meals for enlisted personnel were more pedestrian than the gourmet meals he served to the officers. "The training I received as a Stewardsman was equivalent to the skill set of a garde-manger, chef-educator, sous chef, pastry chef—or even an executive chef in a civilian workplace."[25]

After serving on several ships and an extensive interview process, De Guzman entered presidential food service, hoping to be assigned to the White House Mess.[26] The "White House Mess" is not a political statement but rather the name for an intimate cooking and dining space in the West Wing. One can trace its origins to an afternoon in 1948 when First Lady Bess Truman hosted a reception for the Daughters of the American Revolution in the White House Blue Room. She noticed the tremendous chandelier swaying under the weight of a hefty butler walking above and was terrified that it was going to fall from the ceiling onto her guests.[27] One thing led to another, an inspection ensued, and the Trumans moved out of the White House until 1952 while the building was extensively renovated.

During the renovation, two significant installations changed the course of presidential food service. White House Usher J. B. West recalled, "With air conditioning, Washington became a year-round city, the White House a year-round house."[28] As continual residence became the norm, the White House suddenly needed more staff. However, West and the Trumans both knew that getting more staff, especially for the refurbished kitchen, was a nonstarter with Congress. President Truman, who mused aloud about where to get kitchen help within earshot of Chief Usher Howard Crim, posited that the only option was military personnel. When West succeeded Crim as chief usher, Mrs. Truman, who had obviously been thinking about the same challenge, said, "Mr. West, I have an idea. We aren't planning to use the *Williamsburg* as much as we have been, now that it's so pleasant up here [presumably due to air conditioning]. Could we bring some of the Filipino stewards in to be housemen and kitchen helpers? Do you think the Navy would approve?" That set the bureaucratic wheels in motion. West reported that "the Navy quietly acquiesced, assigning three seamen to the White House pantry and as housemen to help with heavy cleaning, vacuuming, waxing, washing walls upstairs."[29]

Beginning with Mrs. Truman, the seamen "became a White House fixture. Some, after they retired from the Navy," said West, "stayed on as White House employees. Until that time, though, the Navy paid their salaries."[30] Some of the Filipino mess attendants were employed as butlers, but most went to staff the newly created dining space in the White House's West Wing called the White House Mess. President Truman's naval aide, Rear Admiral Robert L. Dennison, had recommended the idea of a mess, and it became official by executive order on June 11, 1951.[31] This navy-run, semiexclusive dining space was immediately denounced as elitist. Critics also pointed out that, though White House staffers paid for their meals, the food often went for below market price.[32]

Bradley H. Patterson Jr. of the Brookings Institution gave a more favorable description of this clubby, private dining room in his seminal work on White House operations:

> *Managed by the navy, the White House Staff Mess consists of three adjacent dining rooms in the lower level of the West Wing that seat forty-five, twenty-eight, and eighteen, respectively, in paneled decorum, for each of the two noonday shifts. Some two hundred staffers and the cabinet are eligible [to dine there]. Dinners are now served as well—a reflection of the lengthening White House workday. Private luncheons in their own offices are available for West Wing senior staff, and carryout trays are provided for harried aides on the run. At the entrance to the mess, hanging noiselessly under glass, is a hallowed symbol: the 1790 dinner bell from the USS* Constitution.[33]

George H. W. Bush visits Chef Ariel De Guzman in the kitchen as he prepares soup for the former president's lunch, 2005.

Significantly, while the White House Mess is located within the White House, it

> is entirely separate from the first family's kitchen and dining facilities in the Residence. The mess and the valets—a staff of fifty—are supervised by the presidential food service coordinator. Those who eat in the mess pay for their food, but the salaries of the navy service personnel are borne by the navy. When the president travels, mess attendants prepare some of the first family's meals, and when the chief executive hosts a dinner during a state visit abroad, mess personnel oversee the food preparation.[34]

While the presidential yacht remained in service, the crew moved back and forth between it and the White House Mess. Sometimes other navy personnel were used to staff the yacht whenever the president wanted to sail.

Since the presidential yacht no longer existed by the time of Ronald Reagan's presidency, De Guzman applied to work in the White House Mess. However, he was soon offered the opportunity to fill a sudden vacancy at the vice president's residence at the Naval Observatory in Washington, D.C. In 1981, he accepted that position and thus began a two-decades-long career of cooking for George H. W. Bush's family.[35]

One of De Guzman's cherished memories is a time when Second Lady Barbara Bush entertained a group of Brownie Scouts at the vice president's house.

Chef De Guzman prepares dessert for former President and Mrs. George H. W. Bush in their Houston home, 2005.

34 COOKING TO THE PRESIDENT'S TASTE

She started with her usual welcome speech, adding information about the house and its historical significance.

She noticed many of the Brownies weren't paying much attention to her speech because Orlando Frilles and I unknowingly distracted them as we set the table with drinks and assorted cookies. She hurriedly finished her speech saying, "This house has a huge kitchen, which is located in the basement of this three-story house, home of the Vice President of the United States. All food prepared from the basement is brought up to this floor by using the dumbwaiter." She then invited everyone to help themselves to the cookies. As I was passing drinks to the little girls, one of them tugged my pants and said, "Mister, I don't care if you're dumb; your cookies are good anyway."[36]

De Guzman's anecdote epitomizes the saying "Out of the mouth of babes ofttimes come gems."

Once George H. W. Bush became president, he hired De Guzman to cook in the White House, the family's Houston residence, the Walker's Point retreat in Kennebunkport, Maine, the George H. W. Bush Presidential Library and Museum in College Station, Texas, and various naval vessels. In the spring of 1994, former President Bush asked De Guzman if he "could break away from the military duty and head to Maine to provide temporary help during the summer." De Guzman inventively flipped the question in a way to get a more permanent job situation. He asked his former boss: "I decided to retire from active military duty, could they use my services?"[37] Bush said yes, and De Guzman filled the position of chef–house manager. No one was happier about this development than Paula Rendon, the Bush family's longtime domestic servant, who was doing everything by herself at 75 years old![38]

De Guzman described the Walker's Point summers as his busy season. With President Bush's extended family frequently visiting, including future President George W. Bush, De Guzman prepared three meals a day, seven days a week. He noted in his cookbook that:

Grandchildren receive different menus from adults and are served at separate hours. I serve vegetarian menus, non-dairy meals, boxed lunches for beachgoers, meals-to-go for the avid boat riders and fishermen, tea for visiting guests, cocktails before dinner, occasional formal receptions, cookouts, meetings, clambakes, birthday celebrations, swimming pool parties, and any last-minute events. I also prepare for the arrival of dignitaries, heads of state, or high officials from across the globe. But no matter how busy my summers get, the thrill I experienced walking into this job is the thrill I receive today. I love my work.[39]

An example of a special meal is what De Guzman called a "Walker's Point Lobster Dinner." The meal featured a whole lobster per person, lemon wedges, a dipping sauce of olive oil and lemon juice, broiled red pepper strips on lettuce beds, baked sweet potatoes, buttered corn on the cob, puffed cheese rolls, and pecan pie.[40]

De Guzman had a distinguished career in presidential food service that, like many before, was singularly tied to a first family. When De Guzman published *The Bush Family Cookbook* in 2005, President George H. W. Bush wrote these words in the foreword:

He has been through all of the ups and downs with me—from the tranquility of Camp David; to that now famous meeting with Mikhail Gorbachev in the stormy seas off Malta; through the turmoil and tension of Iraq's invasion of Kuwait, followed by the triumphant end of Desert Storm; and then of course the 1992 election. . . .

I am so glad that Ariel has decided to share his story, not to mention his great recipes, with all of you. His is truly a great American story.[41]

President Bush's words serve as a testament to De Guzman's culinary excellence and their friendship, and as an appropriate benediction to this chapter on the many ways that cooks serve a president, in almost all roles except for the White House executive chef position, which has always been the most visible aspect of presidential food service and one that we will examine in the next chapter.

CHAPTER FOUR

AT THE HELM IN THE WHITE HOUSE KITCHEN

Food is really the best diplomatic tool of all. Just as with families and friends, you're at a communal table. . . . It's the same for the first family. When they entertain and the way they entertain, it says, "This is how we show love. This is the love of food."
—CRISTETA COMERFORD

White House Executive Chef Cristeta Comerford prepares dinner for the Prince of Wales, 2005.

AT THE HELM IN THE WHITE HOUSE KITCHEN

Chef Pedro Udo at work in the White House Kitchen, c. 1961.

38   COOKING TO THE PRESIDENT'S TASTE

While presidential food service comes in many forms, the one that has most fascinated the public is the cooking that happens in the northwest corner of the Ground Floor of the White House. That is the location of the Executive Mansion's main kitchen, where it has been since First Lady Mary Todd Lincoln moved it from the center of the basement.

PEDRO UDO

Now we meet Pedro Udo, the very first Asian heritage chef to fully helm the White House Kitchen. He got the job with the culinary professional equivalent of a "battlefield promotion." Born in Ponging Signon in the Philippines, Udo served twenty-eight years in the U.S. Navy and was noted for his excellent service record. He retired as a chief steward after serving aboard the USS *Yosemite*.[1] Udo married Jeannete Yeren in 1951, and they had six daughters and two sons.[2] After his retirement, Udo was tapped by White House staffers who prioritized recruiting military-trained cooks, and they were certainly impressed by Udo's stellar service record in the navy. He was first hired as a meat chef.[3]

Udo's opportunity arose when François Rysavy, the previous chef, a naturalized citizen who had been born in what was then Czechoslovakia, abruptly retired in 1957 from the position after only two and a half years of serving President and Mrs. Dwight D. Eisenhower. Gossip columnists speculated that Rysavy's motive was egotistical as well as financial. He felt that his $5,100 annual salary (a little more than $57,000 in 2025 dollars) was far too low for a man of his talents. Rysavy figured that he could make a lot more on the open market as either a private chef for a wealthy client or by working at a hotel. Rysavy also had a memoir cookbook in the works, and the royalty checks alone would likely dwarf his White House paychecks.[4] With Chef Rysavy's resignation, on June 1, 1957, Pedro Udo was promoted from meat chef to head chef.

However, Chef Udo's tenure got off to a seemingly embarrassing start. On June 9, 1957, President Eisenhower topped off his dinner with some blueberry pie. All seemed well until later that night when Major General Howard McCrum Snyder, Eisenhower's personal doctor, was summoned to the White House at 10:30 p.m. because the president complained of feeling nauseated. Sure enough, he vomited three times during the night. The next morning, the president's queasy condition caused great concern since memories lingered of his heart attack in 1955. Newspapers across the country blared front page headlines like "President Sick with Stomach Upset; Blueberry Pie Blamed as Ike Comes Down Ill."[5] Even the stock market fell sharply because of the news.

Since the episode involved politics at the highest level, finger-pointing ensued and nerves were shaken. Some blamed Rysavy for the fiasco, but he had an alibi: his resignation was effective at the end of May. Udo was never publicly linked to the blueberry pie, so his job was never in jeopardy. In the end it was determined that Eisenhower's condition was not due to food poisoning; instead, the pie was so good that the president simply ate too much of it.

A *National Geographic* profile of the White House further piqued the public's fascination with the White House Kitchen by featuring it in an extensive and vividly illustrated piece published toward the end of the Eisenhower presidency. As one of the staff reporters gushed:

> *Today's White House Kitchen, off the ground floor's arched, portrait-lined corridor, is a cook's dream of stainless steel and white enamel. In it I saw choppers, mixers, grinders, slicers, juicers, coffee roasters, electric ovens, freezers, and a spice cabinet. Only one chef-capped man was in sight. But it was not hard to imagine the bustle when a major dinner is scheduled. The State Dining Room holds at most only 106 guests. But there may be six or seven courses. So serving calls for perfect preparations and split-second timing. The large, informal teas and garden parties are simpler. For these the staff makes cookies and sandwiches, about three for each guest.*[6]

That sole figure identified in the article was Chef Udo, who was plenty busy most days. The Eisenhowers loved to entertain, and beyond the numerous meetings, meals, luncheons, and teas hosted on a day-to-day basis, they gave more State Dinners—seventy—than previous administrations.

One of Chef Udo's earliest high-profile meals occurred on October 17, 1957, when he cooked for Great Britain's Queen Elizabeth II and Prince Philip. The next day the *Atlanta Journal* published the following menu: chilled fresh Hawaiian pineapple, cream of almond soup, broiled filet of English sole, roast Long Island duckling with appropriate vegetables, frozen Nesselrode cream and brandied sauce, demitasse, petits fours.[7] Another momentous meal Chef Udo prepared was for Soviet Premier Nikita Khrushchev during the height of the Cold War in September 1959. According to a newspaper report, the menu included:

> *Melon with prosciutto ham, followed by curry soup with whole wheat melba toast. Crab Louis with cole slaw in a tomato basket and Boston brown bread sandwiches. Roast young turkey accompanied by corn bread dressing, gravy, whole cranberry sauce, scalloped sweet potatoes and pineapple, French green beans amandine and bread sticks. Tossed bibb lettuce, Parmesan topped by "green goddess" dressing and toasted sesame crackers followed by the turkey. In the last spot came lime glace with lady fingers and nuts, candies and coffee.*[8]

In each case, Chef Udo worked closely with First Lady Mamie Eisenhower and the U.S. State Department to create the menus.

Outside of the public eye and press scrutiny, President Eisenhower hosted private "stag dinners" for small, eclectic groups of men, usually about eighteen. When a guest arrived at the White House, the Secret Service escorted him to the Second Floor oval study, where the president personally extended greetings and introduced him to the other guests whom the president had broken into smaller conversation circles of three or four. A waiter would offer beverages for this socializing time. After about 45 minutes, the group headed to the State Dining Room for a five-course dinner accompanied by two to three wines. As Sherman Adams, a former assistant to the president, recalled in his memoir, "Toward the end of the meal the conversation became more general and the president often brought to the attention of the whole group at the time a single topic that interested him and on which he

Chef Pedro Udo is seen second from right as First Lady Mamie Eisenhower visits the White House Kitchen to plan a dinner menu, 1958.

40   COOKING TO THE PRESIDENT'S TASTE

wanted to seek everybody's opinion."⁹ If the president did not cook himself, Chef Udo was responsible for those meals.

Chef Udo stayed on as the Eisenhower presidency transitioned to the Kennedy presidency. He was in charge of all cooking, including preparing small family meals. Legendary White House correspondent Helen Thomas described how First Lady Jacqueline Kennedy set the culinary tone by giving Udo "the recipe card file and cookbooks she had in the kitchen of her Georgetown home." Of note were recipes for fish chowder (JFK's favorite), baked seafood casserole, and hot fruit dessert.¹⁰ Yet the good times in the Kennedy kitchen lasted only so long, for Mrs. Kennedy wanted to take presidential cuisine in a different direction. Much like his early days on the job, Chef Udo was unwittingly involved in a media controversy. Coincidently, the intrigue involved another Asian heritage chef.

Newspaper gossip columnists were abuzz with news that First Lady Jacqueline Kennedy wanted to hire a new executive chef. The rumored new chef was Bui Van Han, a highly regarded Vietnamese chef who was cooking for the French Embassy in London. The political intrigue surrounding Bui Van Han's possible hire was as thick as President Kennedy's beloved chowder. The press could not get straight answers from White House staffers on whether an offer was extended. White House Social Secretary Letitia Baldrige supposedly wrote to the chef, in French, to thank him for his interest and tell him that he would not be getting the job. Chef Udo's only public comment was, "I know nothing about it, and I cannot give you any information about him." No wonder one newspaper headline described the situation as "L'Affaire Bui."¹¹

On March 25, 1961, Chef Udo's stint as head cook ended when René Verdon, a French-born chef acclaimed for his work at the Essex House in New York, reported for duty. Mrs. Kennedy tapped him based on recommendations from Kennedy family friends. Also going forward, at her imperative, the person in charge of presidential cuisine would now have the title White House Executive Chef, and Verdon would be the first to fulfill that role. Even so, Chef Udo remained in the White House Kitchen, but, instead of cooking for the first family, he was assigned to cook for the Residence staff.

During Chef Udo's tenure, African Americans dominated the Residence staff, and this influenced what he cooked. Former White House Chief Usher J. B. West wrote in his memoir of the Black staffers: "They selected their own menus—not chili or pâté, but plain American Southern-style cooking: fried chicken, pork chops, pigs' feet, cornbread, blackeyed peas. They ate family style, in the help's dining room, in the lower basement."¹² Thus Chef Udo learned to become a soul food chef!

Before retiring from presidential food service in the early 1960s, Chef Udo also became familiar with a more unsavory piece of White House Kitchen lore. Chief Usher West vividly described a scene initiated by Mary Kaltman, President Lyndon Johnson's food coordinator:

One day, [she] called me, all alarmed.

"We are missing a ham down in the servants' kitchen," she stated. "I bought a whole ham to feed the extra help we hired for tonight's party, and now it's gone. Somebody stole it!"

"Do you have any suspects?" I asked.

"No, but I think you ought to have everybody searched as they leave tonight."

I didn't, of course, ask the police to search our employees. I did ask Piedro [sic] Udo, who cooked for the domestics, to keep a closer watch on things from then on.

About a month later Udo called, asking for help.

"There's an awful stink in the help's dining room. It's like something dead. I think it's in the walls."

Shades of Edgar Allan Poe, I thought, calling in the engineers and plumbers.

"Here it is," cried "Red" Arrington, as he pried away a section of wall underneath the sink.

The offending item—even more pungent as it was brought into the air—was a well-chewed ham bone!

"Your mystery is solved," I explained to Mary. "The rats dragged the ham off the counter and carried it away."

"Rats!" the housekeeper screamed in horror. "Rats in the White House?"

*"Well, we're in the middle of downtown Washington," I told her. "And don't be alarmed. It's not the first time we've had rats."*¹³

Mrs. Eisenhower does a taste test in the White House Kitchen as Chef Pedro Udo (right) and Butler Charles Ficklin (left) observe.

West gave only part of the story. There are numerous historical accounts of vermin in the White House basement. In fact, things were so bad in the late 1800s that First Lady Caroline Harrison unsuccessfully pushed for the White House to be either relocated or razed and rebuilt. As presidential historian William Seale noted, "The White House was attractive to rats from the start." Over the centuries, cats, the Department of Agriculture, the General Services Administration, the National Park Service, and private extermination companies (equipped with mousetraps and poison) were enlisted in the war against the rats. Yet, despite these efforts, Seale concluded, "Rats and mice are thus an ongoing story at the White House."[14] Thankfully, the rodent problem is far less of a problem today.

More appetizingly, Chef Udo was known for his baking skills, especially cakes. Udo so endeared himself to First Lady Mamie Eisenhower that she was moved to write this letter to him from her Gettysburg farm in July 1957:

> *The president and I wish to thank you for the wonderful cake which you decorated for our 41st wedding anniversary. The basket of the pink rosebuds in the center and the two little doves on the handle of the basket were truly lovely. As for the lacy hearts in each corner and the innumerable flowers, it seemed impossible that these were made of icing and not real. The plaques were very unique also, and I am sure Gen. and Mrs. Heaton enjoyed this beautiful cake fully as much as the president and I. Our warmest thanks for adding such a pleasure to our celebration. With best wishes, Mamie Doud Eisenhower.*[15]

Here Mrs. Eisenhower fully appreciates a culinary artist at the height of his powers. This letter would become one of Chef Udo's most prized possessions from his White House days.

Thanks to Mrs. Eisenhower's enthusiastic cheerleading, Udo "was decorating cakes for bazaars, for her personal friends and members of the family."[16] A newspaper article in 1965 describing a wedding cake featuring pink orchids, created by Udo, was one of the last press mentions for the chef.[17] In 1976, Udo moved from Alexandria, Virginia, to Casselberry, Florida, and died in March 1981 at age 70.[18]

42   COOKING TO THE PRESIDENT'S TASTE

Chef Pedro Udo places a birthday cake for an Eisenhower grandchild in the dumbwaiter near the Ground Floor Kitchen.

AT THE HELM IN THE WHITE HOUSE KITCHEN

CRISTETA PASIA COMERFORD

Nearly a half century passed before another Asian heritage chef earned the opportunity to helm the White House Kitchen. That exceptional chef was Cristeta Pasia Comerford.[19] Comerford was born and raised by food-loving parents in a large middle-class household located in the university district of Manila, Philippines. She helped her mother, a seamstress, cook for a household of more than a dozen people. Comerford explained, "You've got cousins and uncles hanging out there. So basically every meal is like a big banquet, and my mother worked full time because she had a dress shop right in the front of the house. So in between managing all of her seamstresses—I think at the time she had three—when it was time to do lunch, she would go in the back, start cooking." Comerford's mother made simple meals: rice, a vegetable and fish or chicken, sometimes with extra potatoes to stretch the meal.[20] Comerford amusingly remembers wondering, "Why are there more potatoes than meat?" Still, her mom's "family meal is better than a restaurant." Even the men of the university district, like her father, enjoyed a reputation for being great cooks.

True to her upbringing, Comerford planned a future career in food, but not the one her parents expected.[21] Back in 1979, her father was the first to encourage her to be a chef. "He said, 'Cris! You should go to Cordon Bleu and be a chef,'" Comerford remembered. "I didn't even know what Cordon Bleu was. He explained to me that it's a cooking school. I said, no, dad, I like the sciences. I'm going to take food technology at the University of the Philippines because it's a very prestigious school. He said again, 'No, you should go to Cordon Bleu.' But I said no."

Comerford got her bachelor's degree in food technology from the University of the Philippines before taking heed of her father's admonition. She studied classic French cooking and came to the United States when she was age 23.[22] She began her career overseeing a salad bar at a hotel near Chicago's O'Hare International Airport and later went on to become chef tournant at Le Ciel in Vienna, Austria, a chef at Le Grande Bistro at the Westin Hotel in Washington, D.C., and a chef at the Colonnade

Executive Chef Cristeta Pasia Comerford poses in the White House Kitchen shortly after her promotion from assistant chef, 2005.

at the ANA Hotel in Washington, where she implemented the "Culinary Arts Gallery" that showcased the best of American fine cuisine.[23] She met her husband, John Comerford, while in Chicago. She said she never considered that nourishing people, and doing a lot with a little, could be a job. But her father did.[24] With a laugh, Chef Comerford acknowledged, "It just proves to you that my father really knew best, because that's what I turned out to be—a chef."

Comerford's first glimpse of the U.S. presidency came when she watched, in person, President George H. W. Bush's Inauguration in 1989. In October 1994, the White House Kitchen needed help preparing President and Mrs. Bill Clinton's State Dinner for Nelson Mandela, newly elected president of the Republic of South Africa, and Comerford was hired as a Service-by-Agreement (SBA) chef, a temporary, independent contract position. After clearing a security background check, these cooks are hired on an as-needed basis, usually for the larger events.[25] Comerford immediately impressed White House Executive Chef Walter Scheib.

"As Cris began to work," Scheib wrote in his memoir cookbook, *White House Chef,* "her tremendous ability became readily apparent. She wasn't a showboat, but was highly organized (her station was a model of efficiency), and she had a great eye and palate. Even the most simple salads were beautiful when she made them, and the vinaigrettes were balanced and seasoned superlatively. Cris's enthusiasm for the White House and professionalism on her job moved her right to the top of my SBA list."[26] Chef Scheib regularly called on Comerford to help out, and as soon as there was an opening, in 1995, he hired her as an assistant chef in the White House Kitchen.

Chef Scheib recognized that Comerford would immediately face a two-fold challenge. First, SBAs are considered "outsiders" since they do not regularly work in the kitchen. Her peers might not readily accept her. Second, she would encounter sexism in a predominantly male workplace. Comerford thrived despite the challenges, and Scheib attributed much of the culinary team's success to her contribution. Scheib wrote enthusiastically, "If I hadn't hired her, a lot of our successes would have been much harder to come by because she had the tremendous ability to hear what I requested, understand its essence, and make it real. Simply put, Cris was the best cook that I had ever cooked with."[27]

In time, President George W. Bush and First Lady Laura Bush wanted a change in the top chef position. When they selected Comerford, Scheib was magnanimous instead of being bitter. "I was thrilled for her when, in August 2005, six months after my departure, Mrs. Bush selected her to be my successor as White House executive chef," Schieb wrote.[28] Comerford, a woman of deep faith, recalled what her pastor taught about a story in Exodus 4 of the Bible. Moses, an elderly, stuttering sheepherder expressed self-doubt when God called him to lead the Israelites out of bondage in Egypt. Comerford was a little apprehensive about accepting the position, but assured herself that she could meet the moment. "God does not call the qualified," she expounded. "He qualifies the call."

By no means did Comerford think that she was unqualified. "Before I got to the White House," she shared, "I had twelve years of experience as a chef, as a sous chef, as a salad girl, be it whatever. But I see everything that happened in my life as a part of the preparation to get to where I was." After she became the first woman and person of color to serve under the title of White House Executive Chef, she likened her early days in that role to an animated movie. "When it was announced in August of 2005 that I was the chef," Comerford said with a laugh, "what comes to mind is, remember the movie *Finding Nemo*? All of those aquarium fishes were plotting to escape to the Sydney Harbor in Australia. And when finally they escaped, they said, 'OK, what is it we're supposed to do?'"

Like her Asian heritage predecessor, Chef Udo, Chef Comerford's first grand culinary spotlight featured British royalty. But in early November 2005, instead of Queen Elizabeth II, it was an official dinner for the Prince of Wales and Camilla, Duchess of Cornwall. Comerford continued the trend started in the Clinton presidency of featuring American ingredients for State Dinners. As an example, the five-course meal included a main entrée of medallions of buffalo tenderloin, roasted corn, wild rice pancakes, glazed parsnips, and young carrots. She also focused on catering to the Bushes' palate for private and public meals "from huevos rancheros, the president's favorite Sunday breakfast, to oysters and spinach au gratin for one of Mrs. Bush's literary-themed dinners, this one honoring Shakespeare."[29] She brought her own style to the White House's 900-square-foot kitchen and encouraged the same in others. At heritage events and even State Dinners, she asked around for family recipes instead of offering her own interpretation of traditional foods like Filipino *lumpia*, Indian *chana puri*, or Greek *dolmas*. "We really tried to do it" the way "somebody's mom or grandma would do it," Comerford said.³⁰

When in spring 2009 First Lady Michelle Obama created the first large-scale kitchen garden on the White House Grounds since the 1870s, it made an impact on menus at the White House. Chef Comerford explained:

*We plan our menus for events, large and small, by what is growing fresh in the garden. Our menus really revolve around nature, around what is out in the garden and ready to harvest. Since we planted the garden, I've noticed a change in what we cook. No longer are the meals we serve driven by the protein on the plate and garnished with a few baby carrots or other accent vegetables. Vegetables are now equal partners. And these aren't the vegetables from our childhoods, cooked until they become mushy and turned a different color. When vegetables are fresh from the garden, you can simply sauté them or cook them lightly and add a few fresh herbs. And in many cases, complementary foods grow at the same time during the season. Tomatoes and eggplant, for example, share the same harvest period and taste delicious together.*³¹

Collard greens harvested from the Kitchen Garden starred on Thanksgiving and at private dinners hosted by the Obamas. For luncheons and large receptions, the Obamas often served a winter salad featuring fennel, pears, and shallots. With an active beehive on the White House Grounds, President Barack Obama used cultivated honey to brew a pale ale that he reportedly unveiled at a private Super Bowl party in 2011.³²

The garden also helped Comerford connect with her daughter Danielle, a competitive gymnast when she was growing up. As a chef and a mother, Comerford wanted to set an example by making smart food choices and putting into practice at home what she learned from the garden at work.³³ The lessons sank in. Danielle got interested in cooking and wound up attending Johnson & Wales University in Providence, Rhode Island, one of the nation's premier culinary schools.

As part of her "Let's Move" initiative, First Lady Michelle Obama created an event called the "Kids' State Dinner" in 2012. It involved a nationwide recipe contest for children between the ages of 8 and 12. A winner was selected from each state and U.S. territory, and in August the winners were invited to the White House's East Room to celebrate their selection and share their experiences. This special dinner happened annually until the Obamas left the White House. For Comerford, it was the event that was the most memorable, fun, and scary. "Kids will say what they think," Comerford observed. "They're very honest people. So you have to make sure the food you make is good. As a chef, I was actually nervous in a weird way. My gosh, I hope they eat food because kids are very finicky." Comerford felt that the dinners went well, but "I think they were being polite because their moms were there," she mused.

Because she cooked for five presidential families, Comerford's culinary style is necessarily eclectic. She supervised a staff of five assistant chefs who worked in different shifts. On a typical day that did not involve a big event, Comerford woke up around 4:30 a.m. and began a daily regimen of elliptical exercise, showering, and quiet time. On the ride from Columbia, Maryland, into work, she listened to her pastor's sermons and Bible study and pivoted to going down her mental list of things to do that day. By 7:00 a.m., she would be ready to work in the White House Kitchen. One of her assistants would have arrived earlier to handle the first family's breakfast, so she would check e-mails and then inspect the kitchen. Thanks to the impeccable job by longtime kitchen steward Adam Collick, she did not have much to worry about on that end. For the most part, little is prepped ahead of time until the cooking is necessary. Sometimes it was just a matter of getting things from the White House Kitchen Garden. The rest of the 10-hour day was filled with cooking and managing. With a young daughter at home, Comerford heavily relied on her husband, John, to maintain a work-life balance. She readily acknowledged the sacrifice that he made to make her career possible.

Comerford also acknowledged that she relied on her senses as a key to success, but not the sense that might come first to mind.

Basically, you have to be cognizant of everything. It's not just about cooking. It's about reading the news, watching the news, watching what's happening, you know, learning your tenants. Your tenants could be there for four years, for eight years, but really listening intently. Then you know what the first family is expecting from you. Because that really starts the whole understanding of what you need to do to execute things that they need and would prefer.

Executive Chef Comerford prepares to use fresh winter greens from the White House Kitchen Garden, 2012.

This is the advice Comerford gives to any aspiring White House chef.

Feeling that it was finally time, Comerford retired in late July 2024. After ten years as an assistant chef and nineteen years as the head chef, Comerford is the longest-serving chef in White House history. The only other chef who comes close is Henry Haller, who was the executive chef for two decades, serving Presidents Lyndon Johnson, Richard Nixon, Gerald Ford, Jimmy Carter, and Ronald Reagan. Looking back on her White House career, Comerford reflected, "I really think this is the most demanding job, but I loved every minute of it."[34] Her father, who first nudged her on this career path, had died in 1991 and never got to see his daughter fulfill her culinary destiny. Comerford wishes she could cook for him just one more time and make something with seafood, which he really loved. "He would have been so proud."

Since U.S. presidents have to earn election, and reelection, and are subject to term limits, the White House Kitchen bears witness to a continual progression of presidential tastes, style, equipment, and even personnel. Thus, save the weight of presidential tradition, the magic of presidential hospitality is that there is no permanent protocol for how things are done. First families can change things up as they see fit. In the next chapter, we will see more examples of how Asian heritage chefs have been involved in creative change at the White House.

AT THE HELM IN THE WHITE HOUSE KITCHEN

CHAPTER FIVE

WHITE HOUSE STAFF CHEFS AND STATE DINNER GUEST CHEFS

I guess my style is whatever the family wants.
—PERMSIN ("TOMMY") KURPRADIT

Chef Permsin ("Tommy") Kurpradit clips rosemary in the East Garden of the White House for use in preparing a State Dinner, 2007.

O ver the years, presidential cooks have taken many paths to the White House Kitchen. Some of these chefs have had prior personal connections with first families before they moved into the White House. Professional reputation or military service, which, as we have seen in previous chapters, is how most Asian heritage chefs got their first opportunity.

JOHNNY PAJE

Irineo Esperancilla's son-in-law, Juanito ("Johnny") Paje, began working at the White House in 1969 during his service in the U.S. Navy when he was assigned to the Navy Mess. After retiring from the navy in 1980, he was hired as a staff chef, a position he held until his death in 2000. The White House staff still remember him today, not only for his cooking, but for his kindness, which was reflected in the meals he prepared. If someone wanted a specific meal prepared a certain way, it was known that Paje would prepare it exactly the way they liked—time and time again. The Residence staff kitchen was named J.P.'s Cafe in his honor when it was renovated in 2022.[1]

Johnny Paje (above), a U.S. Navy recruit from the Philippines, prepared food in White House kitchens for more than thirty years. From 1969 to 1980, he served in the Navy Mess (seen in 2024, top) and from 1980 until 2000 he was a staff chef in the Residence.

50   COOKING TO THE PRESIDENT'S TASTE

SUSAN LIMB

As a Service-by-Agreement (SBA) staff chef, Susan Limb had a front-row seat to the wondrous world of desserts created by longtime White House Pastry Chef Roland Mesnier.[2] Her journey to the White House was quite unexpected. Limb had an unusual childhood by American standards, but not for Asians. Her parents were living in southern California when her mother found out she was pregnant with twins. Her father's demanding profession required extensive travel around the world, and he was often away from the family. This situation left her mother needing extra help and an environment with additional support to care for her children. Limb's mother traveled home to her native South Korea, where she gave birth to Limb and her twin sister. Limb's grandparents were enlisted to help raise them, and her parents shuttled back and forth between the United States and South Korea for the first two years of Limb's life. After that, she was permanently reunited with her parents in Los Angeles and spent the rest of her childhood there.

After high school, Limb enrolled in the University of California, Irvine, and majored in biological sciences and history in preparation for medical school. However, after volunteering in doctors' offices and seeing firsthand the control health insurance companies exerted in the health profession, Limb had a life-changing revelation. "I did not want to go to med school if this was the future of medicine," Limb said. She did not expect her parents to take the news well, but they surprised her. "They were actually very supportive. Culinary arts was not a field my parents wanted me to go into, but they never pressured my sisters or me with their own personal expectations, so I should not have been surprised. To them, it was always, 'Did you give your best effort?' and if we did, that was good enough for them." Limb admitted, "They are very atypical Asian parents."

A couple of months after graduation, Limb soon learned that her parents' understanding about her career plans had limits. Limb's mother suggested that Limb go stay with her twin sister, who was enrolled in a college semester program in Washington, D.C. That was all it took for Limb. Growing up in southern California filled with mostly sunny days, there was not much variation in the weather, let alone the seasons. "Coming here in the fall and seeing the leaves change was such an experience for me. And seeing Mount Vernon and Old Town Alexandria, which had been established more than two

During her time as a Service-by-Agreement staff chef, Susan Limb is seen with her colleagues from the White House Pastry Shop. Left to right, Chef Limb, Executive Pastry Chef Roland Mesnier, Susan Morrison, Lynn McCartin, Marlene Roudebush, and Patrick Musel.

Chef Limb, third from the right, joins White House pastry chefs in the East Room beside a holiday dessert buffet of their creation. The display is filled with cookies, pastries, fruits, and a large eagle of molded chocolate, 2002.

hundred years ago, fascinated me as a history major."

Limb immediately started thinking about how to get back to the nation's capital. In fall 1996 she settled on going to Georgetown University for a graduate degree while living in Washington and contemplating her next steps. The graduate program that interested her the most was geared toward working professionals, so the classes were held in the evening. Since she would be free during the daytime, her love of cooking made taking some culinary courses an attractive option. Limb recalled, "I've always loved cooking. My family traveled extensively while I was growing up, anywhere from Europe to South America to East Asia and Southeast Asia. That was what our summers were all about. My mom said that every time we went to any country, I would always go look for the cookbooks. Whether we were in Hong Kong, Italy, or wherever, I would go look for the cookbooks as a kid."

Flipping through an issue of *Bon Appetit*, Limb noticed a full-page listing of culinary schools. "And I was looking and there was a phone number for this place called L'Académie de Cuisine," she said. "The phone number had the same area code as where I was so I thought it can't be far. Maryland is not very big." She located the school, and, after a little investigation, she decided that it would be too much to do the full culinary program and continue to be in graduate school at the same time. "I just wanted to do it for fun," she said. "I enrolled in the pastry program because it met only a couple days of the week and worked with my school schedule."

Limb saw her future in the art of layered dough. "We started off with the basics such as *pâte à choux*, which was the first thing we made," she recalled. "When we completed that lesson, we moved on to laminated dough and made croissants. And the day we made croissants, I thought, That's it. This is the coolest thing. Not everybody can make a croissant. This was in the age before YouTube so it was difficult to teach yourself." Limb enjoyed the experience so much that she often volunteered at the culinary school when she had extra time.

Like others before her, Limb's path to the White House Kitchen came through a professional connection. Mark Ramsdell, pastry instructor, had been an assistant to longtime White House Pastry Chef Roland Mesnier. Ramsdell, with a doctorate in engineering, provided invaluable structural assistance to Mesnier during the construction of the annual White House Christmas gingerbread house, a signature project under Mesnier's direction. For many reasons, the Clintons decided to ramp up the number of events they planned to host. Mesnier, now in desperate need of additional help to satisfy all the sweet tooths coming their way, turned to Ramsdell for referrals. Ramsdell, in turn, recommended Limb for one of the temporary, part-time jobs.

Unforgettable events marked Limb's early experiences at the White House, including a National Endowment for the Arts function in June 1998 and the Fiftieth Anniversary celebration of the North Atlantic Treaty Organization (NATO) a year later. For the former, Limb recalled a particularly intricate task. "Chef Mesnier had piped tiny details with chocolate," Limb remembered, "so I had a little spatula, and my job was to lift each detail off the parchment without breaking it. It was very nerve-racking." Despite the high-pressure environment, Chef Mesnier was intentional about creating a hospitable and supportive work environment. Limb noted that, given all the repetitive and arduous tasks he asked of his assistants, he "often helped, working right alongside us—pitting cases of cherries together comes to mind. He always made sure everybody had enough time for a break. He was mindful of that."

Many a time Limb found herself in awe of Chef Mesnier's creative process—watching ideas evolve from meticulous research to finished masterpiece. "Roland was always very attentive to unique details that would lend the creations a personal touch," she said. "I still remember the State Dinner that Roland did for Morocco. He visited the Moroccan Embassy, noticed a design on the walls, and decided to incorporate it into his dessert." For another State Dinner, Mesnier made a little chocolate Japanese footbridge with a kiwi pond for each plate. During the George W. Bush presidency, a Baseball Hall of Fame event featured a baseball mitt made of tuile cookies, "and then we piped the netting of the baseball mitt in chocolate. We then made hollowed-out meringue baseballs filled with passion fruit mousse and the red stitching added on all the balls." For a State Dinner for India, "guests enjoyed a lotus flower with each petal delicately fashioned out of chocolate."[3]

Yet for all the wonder, one Mesnier dessert stood out above the others for Limb, even though it was served at multiple events. "I still dream about Roland's peach and blackberry cobbler. It was my absolute favorite dessert that we made. We frequently served that when the Clintons hosted events on the South Lawn."

Limb did contract dessert work through the 2005 holiday season, sometimes working alongside Susan Morrison, who became the White House Executive Pastry Chef a few years after Roland Mesnier retired. In 2006, Limb and her business partner, Patrick Musel, whom she met while working at the White House, opened the highly acclaimed Praline Bakery in Bethesda, Maryland. Despite the immense popularity of baking and desserts on social media and television, Limb does not chase fads. "I tend to be more tried and true. And I know there are a lot of really cool things out there, but at the same time it's a phase, a fad, and I've never been one to chase that. For me, consistency is key, so we don't change our recipes. We now have customers who have been coming here since they were born, and they remember the cookies they had as a child. They know the cookies will taste the same now as they did eighteen years ago. To me, that is what makes all the difference."

Soon after Limb's departure, change came to the White House in an interesting and innovative way. The Obamas hosted a State Dinner for Prime Minister Manmohan Singh of India, and rather than have Executive Chef Cristeta Comerford supervise the meal, they gave that honor to celebrity chef Marcus Samuelsson. Limb's mentor Chef Mesnier, as a former White House employee, was very displeased. He felt that the guest chefs would leverage their White House experience for more exposure. "To me, it's a slap in the face. It's an insult," he said.[4] However, Comerford graciously said in an interview for a widely syndicated Associated Press newspaper article that "she appreciates the talented chefs who visit her kitchen and thinks the exchanges make for good meals. 'Their different style and their repertoire, it's really good to see that,' Comerford said. 'Seeing the way they work, the message and technique they offer, it's really a great thing for us.'"[5]

Guest Chef Anita Lo (second from right), with (left to right) Executive Pastry Chef Susan Morrison, Guest Sous Chef Mary Attea, and Executive Chef Cristeta Comerford, listens as First Lady Michelle Obama thanks the chefs for the meal during the State Dinner for Chinese President Xi Jinping, 2015.

ANITA LO

Anita Lo is a first-generation Chinese American. She was born in Detroit and grew up in Birmingham, Michigan, where her family fostered her interest in food. While earning a degree in French language at Columbia University, she studied at Reid Hall, Columbia's French-language institute in Paris. She fell in love with the food culture there and vowed to return. After moving back to the United States, Lo accepted her first kitchen job as garde-manger at Bouley in New York City.

After a year she moved back to Paris and enrolled in École Ritz Escoffier, a revered culinary institution. She received her degree, graduating first in her class with honors, while interning under Guy Savoy and Michel Rostang. Back in New York City, Lo continued to hone her craft at highly regarded restaurants such as Chanterelle and Mirezi. Beginning in 2000, Lo opened her own series of critically acclaimed restaurants in New York, including Annisa, Bar Q, and Rickshaw. Lo has written two cookbooks: *Cooking Without Borders* (2011) and *Solo: A Modern Cookbook for a Party of One* (2018). Chef Lo was also knighted by the French government to the Order of Agricultural Merit. All of Chef Lo's restaurants have now closed, and she focuses on leading international culinary tours with a company called Tour de Forks Travel.[6]

In 2015, when the Obamas invited Lo to prepare the meal for the visiting Chinese President Xi Jinping and his wife Peng Liyuan, she became the first woman to be a guest chef for a White House State Dinner. The dinner was served on September 25, 2015. The following is her account.[7]

TIMING IS EVERYTHING IN COOKING. When there is too little or too much time to execute a dish, things are bound to go wrong. There were many of these pitfalls on the road to what was perhaps the most important dinner of my career. Time, in this case, was decidedly not on my side.

In late August 2015, when I received an e-mail asking me to cook for a State Dinner at the White House, I thought maybe it was a practical joke. I had always wanted to cook there ever since my colleague Marcus Samuelsson had prepared President Obama's first State Dinner, but I was reluctant to get excited until I "Googled" the person who e-mailed me. Sure enough, it was someone in the White House! The State Dinner would be for China's President Xi Jinping on September 25, and I was asked to create a meal that had both American and Chinese influences. I had three days to come up with twelve recipes that fit into that category and could work for a large banquet. Fragile items like my signature foie gras soup dumplings were way too risky. From those twelve recipes, First Lady Michelle Obama would pick the final four courses. While I am Chinese American, I actually didn't have many recipes that fit into the requested flavor profile, and there was no way I was going to attempt a dish that was not tried and true.

When I got the request, I was just about to leave for a trip to India for some culinary-focused charity events, and when I returned, I was still running Annisa, my restaurant in Greenwich Village, New York, where I was the sole owner. Somehow, I got it done using recipes from decades prior in addition to what I had developed more recently. Since there was so little turnaround to plan the menu and test recipes, I sent my sous chef, Mary Attea, to do the high-stakes tasting with the White House staff in Washington. Many of these dishes she had never seen before, but I wasn't worried. Chef Mary has innate talent and an exceptional palate. She later earned a Michelin Star while helming the kitchen at The Musket Room and is a part owner of the hot new restaurant Raf's—both of which are in New York City. She handily accomplished the task. The final menu that I created was wild mushroom soup with Shaoxing wine and black truffle; butter-poached Maine lobster with spinach, shiitake, and leek rice noodle rolls; grilled loin of Colorado lamb with garlic fried milk and *gai lan* (Chinese broccoli); and warm poppyseed bread and butter pudding with Meyer lemon curd for dessert.

I traveled to Washington a few days before the State Dinner to prepare with the White House Kitchen staff, and Chef Mary joined me later, a day before the event. We had plenty of time to properly produce the meal. The White House Kitchen staff was warm, welcoming, and highly skilled, and the kitchen, while small, was very well equipped. The only problem I ran into while preparing the meal was with some of the ingredients. Whoever provisioned the meal purchased the wrong kind of Shaoxing wine, the truffle juice did not taste like much despite being from the true black truffle, *Tuber melanosporum*, and I did not have enough oyster sauce and could not get more. To be fair, chefs are perfectionists, and I am no exception, but it was pretty much all good until the day of the event.

I felt confident that day, despite the fact that the White House team had warned me on several occasions that the evening was not about me. I figured I understood that, as I've always tried to be humble and always valued teamwork. Plus, I understood that this was, first and foremost, a political event. As such, the kitchen had to be ready to go two hours before the scheduled start time, just in case President Obama deemed it necessary to start early. So my rice noodle rolls and perfectly grilled lamb loins went into the hot boxes to heat up and sit for two and a half hours before being served. Unfortunately, by the time they hit the table, the spinach in the rolls was a brownish green and the noodles were breaking into smaller pieces. My perfectly cooked lamb was then perfectly gray and well done instead of an intended medium rare. The bread pudding on the other hand, which was supposed to be warm and would have been OK for that long in a hot box, had to be cycled in because of space restrictions. Ultimately, most of the desserts were served cold. The soup was the only course that I was generally happy with (despite that truffle issue).

We executed the service to where guests were seated from a small side room set up with four folding tables and four hot boxes. Each table was an assembly line for the same dish. In the end, some 250 people were served four courses in 35 minutes. As you can imagine, on top of everything else, the plating was imprecise at best. So many thoughts raced through my mind. I still do not know if they had to keep that pace because President Xi and his team needed to get on a plane to New York, the conversation had taken a bad turn, or the food just was not good enough. Did my culinary diplomacy fail? Today relations between China and the United States seem more strained than they were when I cooked that dinner. Could my meal somehow have played a part in that? I found some solace in words I heard at the beginning of the evening: it was not about me.

After the dinner I was introduced to the room of guests along with Chef Mary and the White House Kitchen staff. To my great relief, everyone applauded and genuinely seemed happy. That was almost ten years ago, and yet I remember that vividly, along with the thrill of getting to meet the Obamas. That is mostly what I think of now when I remember that great honor. Ultimately, time is kind. It heals and gives one of life's greatest gifts—perspective. In the second part of this book you'll find a selection of my State Dinner recipes. They work if you take your time to read them through and follow the instructions. Just do not try to put everything in a hot box for a few hours before serving!

EDWARD LEE

Chef Edward Lee has been described as "one part Southern soul, one part Asian spice, and one part New York attitude."[8] His journey to being a guest chef in the White House Kitchen began in Brooklyn and took him through New York City, Louisville, Kentucky, and Washington, D.C.

Lee knew he did not want to pursue a career that utilized the literature he learned in his degree from New York University. He decided to pursue a culinary passion that he nurtured during his childhood while cooking alongside his grandmother. After training in various restaurants, and at age 25, Lee opened his first restaurant, Clay, an Asian-focused concept in New York City. Lee closed that restaurant after the tragic attacks on September 11, 2001. Earlier that year Lee had fallen in love with Louisville, Kentucky, after a road trip to attend the Kentucky Derby. He soon moved there and began working at 610 Magnolia, a restaurant that he would eventually own and operate himself. Also in Louisville, Lee later opened MilkWood, a restaurant whose menu fused southern comfort food with Asian cuisine. Starting in 2015, Lee opened two locations of Succotash in the Washington, D.C., area. Lee described the Succotash menu as something where he "brings his Korean roots and Southern repertoire to a soulful Southern menu."[9]

In addition to his restaurants, Lee keeps busy these days with numerous projects. He has authored *Smoke & Pickles: Recipes and Stories from a New Southern Kitchen* (2013); *Buttermilk Graffiti: A Chef's Journey to Discover America's New Melting-Pot Cuisine* (2018), a James Beard Award–winning memoir cookbook; and *Bourbon Land: A Spirited Love Letter to My Old Kentucky Whiskey, with Fifty Recipes* (2024). Lee has also appeared on numerous television shows, including the Public Broadcasting System's *Mind of a Chef* (2014), the documentary film *Fermented* (2017), and the hit South Korean competition show, *Culinary Class Wars*.[10]

Despite his busy endeavors, Lee takes time to give back to his community. In 2015 he founded the LEE Initiative to prepare a diverse workforce for the hospitality industry. According to the organization's website, there are two active programs: the Women Chefs Initiative, a six-month leadership development program for women chefs, and the Smoke & Soul Initiative, a forty-week immersive restaurant mentorship program for young adults. In order to meet an immediate need, the organization operated a community kitchen to provide nourishment during the COVID-19 pandemic. Since 2020, the organization has collaborated with the Heinz Corporation and Southern Restaurants for Racial Justice to create the Black Kitchen Initiative, which grants funds to Black-owned food businesses around the country.[11]

With all these accomplishments, it is not surprising that President Joe Biden invited Chef Edward Lee to prepare the State Dinner for South Korean President Yoon Suk Yeol on April 27, 2023. Here is Chef Lee's reminiscence of that occasion.[12]

IN THE COURSE OF A CHEF'S CAREER, we are asked to do many important dinners for clients that can range from celebrities to dignitaries to loved ones celebrating a special day. In the end, though, we are accustomed to the fact that despite the level of VIP involved, it is just food and the logistics of sending out plates of hot food; be it forty or four hundred, it is a pretty standard affair. But nothing could have prepared me for the experience of being the guest chef for a White House State Dinner. From the first moment of receiving an e-mail to the introductory Zoom calls to the tasting with the first lady to the day of the event and the after-party, it was as memorable as anything I have ever done in my career as a chef.

As the child of immigrants who came to America in 1972, I remember the struggles of growing up in a humble, working-class family in Brooklyn. I remember the feeling of being a part of the newest immigrant group and having to find our own path in a land full of immigrants, all with their own unique stories. My parents worked very hard to raise a family in Brooklyn. We did not have much, but we were always taught to be grateful for what we did have. Like most immigrant children, I had to find my own definition of what it meant to be an American. It was not always easy, and I was not always confident in my own identity. But despite it all, I had a pretty American upbringing filled with Coney Island hot dogs and ham and cheese sandwiches, albeit with a side of kimchi always within reach.

When I made the choice to become a chef, it was a difficult day for my mother, who worried that my career path would be filled with little pay and hard hours. She was not wrong, but I did have a satisfying life in the kitchen. My path as a chef would be full of bumps but also full of incredible peaks that validated who I was both as a chef and as a Korean American. I always tried to merge my two identities through my food. So it was a full

Guest Chef Edward Lee at work in the White House Kitchen ahead of the State Dinner for South Korea, 2023.

Guest Chef Edward Lee is flanked by Executive Pastry Chef Susan Morrison, left, and Executive Chef Cristeta Comerford, right, as he explains the menu for a State Dinner in honor of South Korea's President Yoon Suk Yeol during a press preview, 2023.

circle moment for me to cook at the White House for the South Korean president and first lady as well as our U.S. president and first lady. It was an incredible moment to celebrate the journey of my parents and myself from Korea to Brooklyn. My mother was beaming with pride. I think all parents of immigrants who come to America at some point wonder if it was the right choice to leave a country that is their homeland for a land of opportunity but a place that is strange and unfamiliar. It was in this moment that I saw my Mom find a validation of all the struggles of our early life in America. And for me, it was a civic duty to give back to a country that has given me so much.

During the preparation of the meal, I often thought about my childhood. I would smirk to myself thinking how in the world could I have ever predicted that a young Korean boy growing up on the streets of Brooklyn would end up cooking dinner for the heads of two nations in the White House. The life of a chef is one that is always in motion and filled with deadlines and a million daily tasks. We do not often have the luxury of quiet reflection, but I made sure to take time in every step of the dinner preparation to stop and appreciate the moment. From being in a room with First Lady Jill Biden discussing the best way to serve a crab cake to standing in the small but perfectly designed kitchen with Chef Cristeta Comerford planning the steps of service, every moment was both familiar and yet elevated.

One of the things that chefs do at every dinner is to choose plateware. Usually it is a mundane affair in which we choose from a paltry selection of plain white round and oval plates that we hope will look nice with our food. When it came to selecting the plateware for the State Dinner, I was floored by the history, the beauty, and the care that was put into selecting the patterns for the plates. Each plate had a history, and Chef Comerford would explain how one set was used in a dinner with the French prime minister and another was used to celebrate an Inauguration. It is wild to tell the story of American history through a set of beautifully matching plateware, but that is exactly what we did in that narrow hallway of the White House Kitchen. It is a moment that I will never forget.

We started with a Maryland crab cake with a julienne of vegetables that represented a kind of slaw: cucumbers, red and yellow bell peppers, and kohlrabi. The dish was finished with a *gochujang* vinaigrette that bridged the East Coast crab cake with the southern-inspired "slaw." The main course was based on a Korean *galbi jjim*, a slow braised beef short rib with soy sauce, garlic, and ginger. We served it with soft Kentucky grits and a pine nut

58   COOKING TO THE PRESIDENT'S TASTE

relish on top. The dessert course was a classic American dessert—an ice cream banana split sundae. But we added a few twists. We used lemon ice cream, bruléed banana, raspberries, and blackberries. And we finished it with a *doenjang* caramel with agave—the sweet sauce and salty, *umami* kick.

I never get nervous before a dinner, and I have cooked for some pretty illustrious clients. But this was different. I was cooking for the leader of the land where I came from and the leader of the place I call home. It was symbolic and meaningful to me in a way that could not compare with any other event that I have done. It was also filled with Secret Service agents so that ramps up the pressure a little bit. The dinner was actually a blur. We plated the food so fast, and it all went out like clockwork. Before I knew it this incredible moment was over. The last of the dessert plates were wiped and swept away by the wait staff team, and I immediately felt a sadness wash over me. I did not want this dinner to ever end. I was Cinderella, and the clock was approaching midnight.

My wife was able to join me for the intimate after-party, where we sat behind President Biden and watched in awe as the president of South Korea sang Don McLean's "American Pie" in front of a room full of dignitaries. Hearing those lyrics echo through the White House walls was the perfect end to an evening that brought my two worlds together. As a chef, it was the honor of a lifetime to be able to contribute to this moment.

A view of the East Room during the State Dinner in honor of South Korea hosted by President Joe Biden and First Lady Jill Biden, 2023.

WHITE HOUSE STAFF CHEFS AND STATE DINNER GUEST CHEFS

PERMSIN ("TOMMY") KURPRADIT

Following Chef Cristeta Comerford's retirement in July 2024, White House Assistant Chef Permsin ("Tommy") Kurpradit was promoted to the executive chef position on an interim basis. Although the promotion took him by surprise, it was the culmination of a lifelong journey that had begun in the kitchen during his childhood.[13] Growing up as the only child of his Thai immigrant parents, first in Oklahoma and later in Maryland, Kurpradit developed a passion for cooking from an early age. The passion arose not from family recipes or elite training, but from the mesmerizing world of the public television cooking shows that he watched. He did not know that doing something he loved would lead to the ultimate job in the White House Kitchen. He was only eight years old. "I was a very curious kid," Kurpradit recalled, "and I didn't appreciate the transformative power of cooking until I watched chefs on TV combine quality ingredients with masterful techniques to create gorgeous dishes."

The many episodes Kurpradit watched inspired him to imagine himself as a chef in his home's kitchen, and he play-acted the role. "From what I remember," he said, "I would gather whatever I could find in our pantry, just take random things, and pretend I was working in the line in a professional kitchen. My mom's kitchen was my restaurant kitchen. I would call out line orders to myself and try to pretend to serve up beautifully planned meals." Kurpradit quickly graduated to cooking real food, and then the kitchen became an experimental culinary workshop. "One day I made such a huge mess just to make chicken fingers and potatoes, but the satisfaction of biting into the crispy and juicy breaded tenders I had made myself more than made up for the cleanup I had to do," he said. His mother would understandably question the value of these cooking sessions when she witnessed the aftermath and waste. "What did you do?" she would ask. These early experiments were a testament to Kurpradit's burgeoning talent and creativity. But no matter how much he may have pictured himself one day joining the esteemed ranks of professional chefs, it was beyond even his imagination that this love of cooking would eventually lead to his taking on the grand challenge of the White House Kitchen. The creative culinary chaos did not last too long. He wasted so much food that he was no longer allowed to "play chef." Yet his curiosity about cooking only grew.

When Kurpradit was 13, he got a real taste of restaurant life. The Woodmont Country Club in Rockville, Maryland, where his father was a longtime employee, hired him as a busboy. Two years later, during a slow night at the club, the curious kid within reemerged, and he asked the chefs if he could help with the prep work. They agreed, and he absolutely loved it. He marveled that someone could actually get paid to do such work. The chefs saw his work ethic in his passion for chopping onions and parsley and recommended him to the restaurant manager for a job in the kitchen. At 15 years old, and still in high school, Kurpradit donned his first chef's coat. It felt really exciting.

Recognizing Kurpradit's interest, a high school guidance counselor recommended that he consider a trade school program in restaurant management at the Thomas Edison High School of Technology. He enrolled, embraced the program, and excelled. "It wasn't really hard. So, after I did all my work, I would always try to learn more. I would literally carry a cookbook with me everywhere," he said. Seeing that, one of his teachers asked him if he was crazy. He said, "No, you're just like me. I'm your best student, you better support me."

After graduating from high school, Kurpradit did not have enough money to attend prestigious culinary schools like the Culinary Institute of America or Johnson & Wales. A Woodmont Country Club co-worker suggested the restaurant management–culinary program at Northern Virginia Community College. It worked well for Kurpradit's situation: it was affordable, he could still work at the country club, and he did not have to be far from his beloved parents. After graduating from the program, he realized he had learned all that he could at the country club. Even the head chef there told him that he should move on. "Like a lot of people, when they're comfortable, they really don't want to change," Kurpradit reflected. "So everyone pushed me to change because this is not your ending, this is your beginning."

The timing was good because the International Monetary Fund hired Kurpradit to help out with a three-day series of events for up to two thousand people. During the events, the fund's head chef introduced Kurpradit to John Moeller, a friend of his who was a sous chef at the White House. Kurpradit's eyes and mind opened wide, and he thought, "The White House has a chef?" It had never occurred to him. From that point, Kurpradit actively pursued every opportunity to show Moeller his culinary skills. The fund's chef, seeing what was going on, offered to put in a good word for Kurpradit with Moeller, but that referral came at a price. "I'd be happy to hook

Chef Tommy Kurpradit at work in the White House Kitchen, August 28, 2020.

you up and give you the number, but you're working for me for a year," said the chef. "This ain't free."

True to his word, the chef connected Moeller and Kurpradit, and he was ultimately hired as a Service-by-Agreement (SBA) chef for the last six months of Bill Clinton's presidency. Kurpradit was initially assigned the grunt work of prepping twenty cases of spinach. He was so grateful that he was not fazed. "OK, sure," he thought, "but at that point you're in the White House so it didn't matter what I was doing." One thing that did matter was observing Chef Cristeta Comerford in her element. "I saw Cris for the first time, and, before that time, I never really worked with females in the kitchen," he remembered. "If there was a female, she would typically be in the salad station or doing desserts. So, after a while, I was noticing what she would do and some of the stuff she would do. And I thought, wow, this is really cool." He fully appreciated the privilege he had to be in the White House Kitchen at that moment.

After his initial White House stint ended, Kurpradit next considered cooking in London, but the unexpected happened. His job interview took place on September 11, 2001, while the tragic terrorist attacks unfolded in the United States. Kurpradit got the job and tried to make a go of it but lasted only a couple of weeks. He returned to the United States to be closer to his parents given all the uncertainty of those times. Still wanting a challenge, he cold-called top restaurants in the Washington, D.C., area for job opportunities. He was eventually hired at Patrick O'Connell's highly regarded Inn at Little Washington in rural Virginia. Kurpradit enjoyed his time at the inn, but he wanted, he said, "to collect top restaurant jobs like baseball cards." He soon moved to New York City to work at Restaurant Daniel owned by famed chef Daniel Boulud.

Even though working in New York City, Kurpradit stayed connected to the inn and filled in from time to time. That proved fortunate. White House Executive Chef Walter Scheib called the inn and asked Kurpradit to come help at the White House with some events. Kurpradit tried to explain that he was already tied up with commitments at the inn, but Chef Scheib told him, "No, you are coming to work with me. I will call Patrick myself." Scheib's confidence in Kurpradit underscores the reputation he had garnered through his work ethic and skill. Kurpradit was soon back at the White House and working intermittently as an SBA chef.

Eight months later, Chef Scheib resigned. Kurpradit suddenly had a front-row seat as Comerford auditioned for the top job. Kurpradit provided any help she needed

Chef Kurpradit at work in the White House Kitchen, 2012.

Chef Kurpradit waves to acknowledge an introduction by President Donald J. Trump during an event in the East Room, 2019.

during that process. Fifteen minutes after getting the job, she called Kurpradit. "You can rest easy now," she reassured him. "You're safe, like *Survivor*." Kurpradit simply responded with "Thank you." Comerford hired Kurpradit as a full-time White House assistant chef in 2005, and he is grateful. "To this day," he said, "I credit Chef Cris for everything I've accomplished up to this point in the White House. When I started, I wasn't married. I didn't have kids. I didn't own a house. My parents were still helping me a little bit, things like that. And then once she gave me the gift of being her assistant, boom, life started."

Kurpradit's proudest moment as an assistant chef came in 2017 when the Prime Minister of Thailand, General Prayut Chan-o-cha, visited the White House for a working lunch. More than just a career highlight, the event was a personal moment that connected his heritage to his professional identity. The Thai ambassador to the United States knew of Kurpradit and offered to introduce him to the prime minister. On the day of the visit, Kurpradit enthusiastically went to the White House's Cabinet Room and welcomed the Thai delegation. They loved seeing someone of Thai heritage on staff, someone who spoke their language. Television stations in Thailand carried footage of Kurpradit with the delegation, and the news quickly spread across the Pacific Ocean and the continental United States to his parents. "My mom called me," Kurpradit said laughingly, "and she said, 'I'm getting so many phone calls.' She just got bombarded with calls from her friends and family and was excited, 'Hey, Tommy's on TV!'" Reminiscent of his childhood make-believe restaurant days, she asked her son, "What did you do?" Kurpradit observed, "I've never seen her so happy before."

Kurpradit's work in the White House Kitchen also boosted his own happiness. Finding love in demanding kitchens is rare, but Kurpradit found a partner in the pastry kitchen. "For chefs," he explained, "building a relationship is very difficult because you're always working." When he saw Susan Limb working on the White House pastry team, he was intrigued. His reaction was, "Oh, cool! Asian girl!" Kurpradit added, "We got to know each other and just went from there." Their shared passion for their craft and the special bond they formed in the White House made their union more meaningful. Kurpradit and Limb were married in 2008, the same day that Jenna Bush had her wedding party at the White House.

At the time of this writing, Kurpradit serves as the interim White House executive chef and will do so until President Donald J. Trump makes his selection in 2025. Kurpradit is at ease and self-aware in his current role. "I never started working there thinking that I was going to be in charge, right?" he said. "But, at the end of the day, it happens." When asked about his culinary style, Kurpradit's poignant answer unites all chefs who have served our first families since George Washington's presidency: "I guess my style is whatever the family wants."

Recipes

Introduction
DEBORAH CHANG

Chef Lee Ping Quan had more than four hundred recipes in his memoir and cookbook *To a President's Taste*, and the first decision I had to make was which ones to include. His recipes were vast in scope and allowed me to peek into the daily lives of presidents and their families who lived a hundred years ago. The longer I spent time with the recipes, the more impressed I was with Chef Quan's abilities. The fact that Chef Quan had the prescience to know what flavors and recipes would endure is a testament to his talent. Many of the flavors, combinations, and cooking methods still exist. Ultimately, I decided to include recipes that were not too difficult to make at home and that people would most likely enjoy today.

I could not imagine making the recipes by hand as Chef Quan and his kitchen staff did. Imagine what Chef Quan could have done with the ingredients and technology we have today! Modern technology and ingredients made me wonder how much I should change each recipe. At what point does the recipe become so different from Chef Quan's original that it's no longer "his"? Was my obligation to be true to what was actually served or make it the best-tasting recipe a home cook can make? If I thought that I could make the recipe taste better, should I? If I had a shortcut, should I use it? Canned oysters and packaged bamboo shoots are more readily accessible, but fresh are even better, and when that's all Chef Quan had, the result would have been more flavorful. Farm-grown tomatoes and freshly laid eggs, instead of our mass-produced versions, may have been bigger than the ones we buy in supermarkets. We add more because we have more, but that's not always better.

Sometimes I felt like I was trying to decipher a puzzle. I had to make many judgment calls. Some recipes required multiple rounds of testing. Ultimately, the answer to my big question of how much I should adapt the recipe was subjective and probably landed someplace in the middle, with the answer of, "It depends." If a recipe didn't work or was too unwieldy for the modern kitchen (or, frankly, if I could not figure it out), I changed it to an easier method. I selected recipes that required the least adaptation. Although I exercised restraint with the savory recipes, to the extent I thought additional seasonings should be added I made suggestions, some of which are added in the headnotes and some directly in the recipe. I wrote the recipes so that they work and are basically good, would give the home cook a sense of satisfaction, and make a tedious weeknight dinner more fun or a dinner party less work. I also took out ingredients that aren't commonly used today or if the combination would not suit modern palates. Bananas should never be in a salad, in any era.

Regardless, I encourage changes. Make changes if you think they will make the recipe taste or work better. Use these recipes as a learning experience and a journey into food history as I did. Be comforted by the fact that a love for food unites—across different cultures and heritages, across the successes and devastations of different historical periods, and across different political parties.

Finally, I have enjoyed being part of this project, and what started out as a simple collaboration with a college friend has turned into something much more important. I am honored to be part of the preservation of Asian American contributions to U.S. history. It's sometimes hard to tell our stories as we are fewer in numbers than other immigrant groups, and we are not homogeneous. The only way to tell our story is to start one by one. Chef Quan's recipes tell his story, and his story is one that defies categorization. Chef Quan's recipes told me how talented he was, that he was an expert in many forms of cooking (Chinese, American, and European), that he loved his craft, and that he served an important role by being so well regarded by the presidents he served.

Starters, Sides, Salads, and Soups

Lee Ping Quan's
EGG ROLLS

Makes 12 egg rolls

INGREDIENTS

1–1½ pounds Chinese boneless barbecue pork, store bought

1 cup water chestnuts, fresh if you can find them, otherwise canned

1 cup bamboo shoots, fresh if you can find them, otherwise packaged or canned

¼ cup green onion

Salt and pepper

1 egg

2 tablespoons Chinese wine or sherry

2 tablespoons soy sauce

1 package of 12 store-bought egg roll wrappers

1 egg + water for egg wash

Vegetable oil for frying

Store-bought egg roll wrappers can be used to save time. We prefer thicker egg roll wrappers instead of the thinner spring roll wrappers. However, either can be used.

Purchase the barbecue pork from a Chinese market. That is much easier than making it at home.

PREPARATION

1. Finely chop the pork, water chestnuts, bamboo shoots, and onions.
2. Combine and season with salt and pepper.
3. Add egg and mix together.
4. Flavor with Chinese wine and soy sauce.
5. Place the square egg roll wrapper in a diamond configuration so that one corner is facing you. Spoon approximately 2–3 tablespoons of filling onto each egg roll wrapper.
6. Roll the corner closest to you over the filling. Gently press down over each side of the filling. Fold the left and right sides of the wrapper toward the middle. Brush the sides with egg wash and seal the ends.
7. Continue tightly rolling the egg roll until it is completely sealed.
8. Pour 3 inches of oil into a shallow frying pan with edges. The oil is ready when it is rippling and slightly bubbles.
9. Fry 3–4 egg rolls at a time, turning occasionally, until lightly browned, approximately 3–5 minutes.
10. Set aside each egg roll on paper towels.
11. Serve each egg roll on its own. No dipping sauce is needed.

Lee Ping Quan's
SHRIMP À LA *MAYFLOWER*

Serves 6–8 people

INGREDIENTS

2 pounds shrimp

1 stalk celery

1 small onion (preferably red)

3 sprigs parsley (can be omitted, but use flat Italian parsley if you choose to use it)

2 tablespoons chili sauce

1 teaspoon Worcestershire sauce

1 tablespoon fine olive oil

1 teaspoon salt

This recipe can be eaten for lunch or as an appetizer. Chef Quan served it with cheese straws, but you can use any white cracker, such as a water wafer or flatbread cracker. It also tastes great on its own.

We didn't make many changes to this recipe, except that we suggest not using parsley as it is overbearing, and we used red onion, which is sweeter than white onion and tastes better raw. We also played with the different chili sauces, and opted for a Korean gochujang *sauce. Sriracha also works well. Use fine or extra-fine olive oil. A citrusy olive oil like lemon or blood orange would work well, too.*

Chef Quan boiled the shrimp first and then peeled them. We opted to peel and then boil them, to save time, and the recipe is written as such.

PREPARATION

1. Rinse shrimp and peel.
2. Drop into salted boiling water until cooked through, approximately 3–5 minutes.
3. Remove from water and let cool.
4. Dice shrimp into small pieces.
5. Wash and dice the celery, onion, and parsley if you use it, and mix together with the shrimp.
6. Add the chili sauce, Worcestershire sauce, olive oil, and salt.
7. Serve with crackers.

Lee Ping Quan's
CHICKEN À LA PRESIDENT
UNITED STATES STYLE

*Serves 4–6 people
(double for party appetizer)*

INGREDIENTS

1½–2 pounds chicken thighs and breasts, skinless and boneless
4 slices bacon, cut in small pieces
2 tablespoons butter
8 ounces fresh mushrooms, sliced and diced by hand or in a food processor
2 green peppers, small-medium size, diced
2 Spanish pimientos, diced
2 tablespoons flour
1 tablespoon sherry
½ cup cream
6 slices white bread (or 1 whole baguette, thinly sliced)
Plenty of salt and pepper to taste

This recipe can be part of a light lunch or a party appetizer. Chef Quan originally served this as an entrée for a light lunch.

Chef Quan's recipe uses "white bread." There are so many types of "white bread" available today. We suggest using a crusty baguette, toasted with olive oil, salt, and pepper if you like.

You can also opt to toss the mixture with 12 ounces of cooked penne pasta (or similar shape) to make it a meal for a family of four. What this recipe then becomes is a creamy chicken and mushroom pasta.

Shredded grocery-bought rotisserie chicken and chicken stock can be used to skip the step of cooking the chicken.

Small sweet peppers of any color can be substituted for Spanish pimientos.

PREPARATION

1. Boil the chicken in a pot until cooked, about 30 minutes.
2. Remove the chicken and cool. Save the water the chicken was boiled in.
3. Dice the chicken.
4. Over medium heat, sauté the bacon until the fat is rendered.
5. Add butter, and then sauté mushrooms, peppers, and pimientos until softened, about 5 minutes.
6. Add flour and sauté for 1–2 minutes.
7. Gradually add the sherry and the water the chicken was boiled in. Finish with the cream.
8. Serve on bread.

Lee Ping Quan's

CHICKEN STUFFING IN MUSHROOMS
POTOMAC STYLE

Makes approximately 24–36 mushrooms depending on size

INGREDIENTS

24 large cremini or white mushrooms
1 tablespoon butter
2 stalks celery, finely diced
1 pound ground chicken
1 teaspoon sherry
Touch of cream (1–2 tablespoons)
1 tablespoon flour
¼ cup chicken stock
Salt and pepper
Vegetable oil for frying
2 eggs, beaten
Touch of cream (1–2 tablespoons)
Bread crumbs or panko
Optional:
  1 teaspoon sage
  1 teaspoon thyme, chopped
  mushroom stems, chopped

These mushrooms are deep fried and delicious. Deep frying does take patience and can be messy, so we have included a baked version as well, which takes significantly less time. You can add sage and chopped thyme to the chicken mixture, if you desire. Another option is to add the chopped mushroom stems to the chicken mixture.

PREPARATION

1. Remove stems from mushrooms and wash thoroughly (or brush dirt off, whatever you choose). There should be a small cavity for the stuffing. If there is not, scrape around the edge of the caps a bit.
2. Dry with a paper towel.
3. In a saucepan over medium low heat, melt butter.
4. Add celery, then chicken, and sauté lightly.
5. Add sherry, cream, flour, and chicken stock. Season with salt and pepper.
6. Cook until chicken is cooked through, for approximately 5 minutes, and then cool.
7. Set up a pot with enough oil to cover each mushroom. The oil is ready when it ripples or when bread crumbs dropped in bubble and float to the top. Keep the oil at medium or medium low.
8. Place a teaspoon of the chicken mixture in each mushroom.
9. Mix the egg and second touch of cream.
10. Dip each mushroom in egg-cream mixture.
11. Sprinkle with bread crumbs.
12. Fry each mushroom until brown and set each aside on paper towels. Keep warm in a low oven, 150°F.
13. Serve with shoestring potatoes (see page 78) or potato chips.

BAKING PREPARATION

1. Preheat oven to 400°F
2. Follow steps 1–6 above.
3. Place a teaspoon of the chicken mixture in each mushroom.
4. Place stuffed mushrooms on a sheet pan.
5. Sprinkle bread crumbs on each mushroom.
6. Bake for approximately 20 minutes.

Lee Ping Quan's
WHITE HOUSE FRIED SHRIMP

Serves 4 people

INGREDIENTS

Salt and pepper
¼ cup flour
1½ pounds shrimp
1 egg
½ cup ice cold water
1–2 cups unflavored bread crumbs or panko (if using panko, crumble with your hands into smaller pieces)
Vegetable oil for frying

The original recipe called for medium "green" shrimp. We were not sure what Chef Quan meant, but the simplest thing to do is to buy peeled and deveined shrimp from the seafood counter. The larger the shrimp, the more visibly appealing once fried. We prefer to leave the tail on, and butterfly the shrimp, but you can choose to clip the tail off and leave whole.

PREPARATION

1. Combine salt and pepper with flour.
2. Coat shrimp with seasoned flour.
3. Beat egg with cold water.
4. Place bread crumbs in a bowl.
5. In a shallow pan, heat 1–2 inches of oil.
6. Dip coated shrimp into egg and then into bread crumbs.
7. Fry the shrimp in oil until lightly browned. Put each shrimp on a paper towel, and keep shrimp warm in a low oven, 150°F.
8. Repeat for the rest of the shrimp.
9. Serve with shoestring potatoes and tartar sauce (see pages 78 and 88).

Lee Ping Quan's
COMBINATION SLICED VEGETABLE SALAD

Serves 8 people

DRESSING INGREDIENTS

1 cup good mayonnaise
1 tablespoon rice wine vinegar
2 tablespoons sour cream or plain yogurt
¼ teaspoon salt
¼ teaspoon ground pepper
1 teaspoon Worcestershire sauce
1 teaspoon chili sauce (sriracha)

SALAD INGREDIENTS

1 pint cherry tomatoes (or 4 large ripe tomatoes)
4 peppers (red, green, orange, or yellow)
1 English cucumber
2 hearts of Romaine lettuce
3 hard-boiled eggs, crumbled (optional)

The original recipe called for fried peppers and blanched and peeled tomatoes, which we omitted. We opted for a cold salad tossed in a creamy dressing. We altered the dressing to be less vinegary, and we used components of Chef Quan's French dressing recipe to save a step. His French dressing (see page 88) can be used as well to make a noncreamy dressing.

Store-bought mayonnaise is fine, as long as you adjust salt and pepper for your taste.

This is a great recipe for a hot day or if you want to bring it to a picnic or potluck. Serve with a healthy protein such as grilled chicken breast or salmon.

DRESSING PREPARATION

1. In a small bowl, whisk the mayonnaise, rice wine vinegar, sour cream, salt, pepper, Worcestershire sauce, and chili sauce together.

SALAD PREPARATION

1. Prepare the vegetables. Halve the cherry tomatoes. Julienne the peppers. Dice the English cucumber. Tear the hearts of Romaine lettuce into small pieces. Put in a bowl.
2. Dress the vegetables before serving.
3. Toss in the crumbled hard-boiled eggs if you choose to use them.

Lee Ping Quan's
CORN FRITTERS
POTOMAC STYLE

Makes 12 fritters

INGREDIENTS

3 cups white or yellow corn, fresh shucked or frozen, thawed and drained
⅓ cup flour
1 egg
¾ tablespoon baking powder
1 tablespoon half-and-half
1 tablespoon salt
½ teaspoon fresh ground pepper
Vegetable oil for pan frying

This dish is a nice alternative to corn on the cob. We increased the flour used in Chef Quan's original recipe, as the batter did not hold together. Chef Quan's original recipe also called for "green corn," which we do not have today, as he may have meant unripe corn, so we used white or yellow corn.

PREPARATION

1. In a bowl, mix all the ingredients together.
2. In a frying pan, heat 2 inches of oil over medium heat until oil is rippling or drop a small dab of batter into the oil. If the batter bubbles lightly and then rises to the top, then the oil is ready.
3. Drop rounded tablespoons of fritter batter into the oil.
4. Fry each side for 1–2 minutes until lightly browned. Flip over. If oil gets too hot too quickly, reduce heat to low.

Lee Ping Quan's
SHOESTRING POTATOES

Serves 4 people

INGREDIENTS

3 jumbo or 4–5 small/medium russet potatoes
Vegetable oil for deep frying
Salt

There is no need to skin the potatoes, as we prefer the look of the potatoes with the skin on. A mandolin or a food processor attachment can be used, but we prefer to hand cut the potatoes into shoestrings. The potatoes can be prepared ahead of time as long as they are stored in water and refrigerated.

PREPARATION

1. Cut the potatoes into long shoestrings. Place in water as you finish.
2. Drain the potatoes and pat dry.
3. Heat a deep fryer to 325°F.
4. Lay out sheet pans lined with paper towels.
5. In batches, deep fry the potatoes for 4 minutes. Place the shoestrings on a paper-towel lined pan. They will be soft looking.
6. Increase the heat of the deep fryer to 375°F.
7. In batches, deep fry the potatoes again in small batches for 2 minutes until lightly browned and crispy. Keep each batch warm in a 150°F oven.
8. Salt to taste.

Lee Ping Quan's

CREAMED CAULIFLOWER
USS *MAYFLOWER* STYLE

Serves 4–8 people

INGREDIENTS

1 head cauliflower, cut into florets only, discarding stalk
2 tablespoons butter (salted or unsalted)
2 tablespoons flour
½ cup cauliflower juice (see steps 2–3)
½ cup cream (you could use half-and-half or whole milk)
1 tablespoon salt
½ teaspoon pepper
Optional:
 ½ teaspoon nutmeg
 1 teaspoon garlic powder
 1 teaspoon onion powder
¼ cup grated cheese (Romano, Parmesan, and/or Gruyère)
Chopped chives for garnish

BREAD CRUMB TOPPING

1 cup bread crumbs
3 tablespoons butter

Our favorite part of this recipe is Chef Quan's reference in the original text to "cauliflower juice," which is the water the cauliflower is boiled in. Reserve it for the sauce. You can adjust the salt and pepper to your taste. You can also add nutmeg, a bit of garlic powder, or onion powder. Think what you would add to macaroni and cheese, or keep it simple with just salt and pepper.

Chef Quan's original recipe called for American cheese. Instead, we recommend using white grated cheese. The original recipe uses the equivalent of 1 ounce of cheese. We quadrupled the amount to increase the flavor.

We added a bread crumb topping to enhance the flavor and texture of the dish.

PREPARATION

1. Preheat oven to 350°F.
2. In a pot of salted boiling water, boil cauliflower until al dente, approximately 5 minutes. Do not overcook.
3. Drain, reserving 2–4 cups of the "cauliflower juice" (water). Set the juice and cauliflower aside.
4. Over low to medium heat, melt butter (but do not brown).
5. Add flour and stir to combine.
6. Increase heat to medium, and slowly add the cauliflower juice and the cream, whisking slowly to eliminate lumps.
7. Continue to stir occasionally until sauce lightly thickens, approximately 3 minutes.
8. Add salt, pepper, and optional nutmeg, garlic powder, and/or onion powder. The sauce will thicken in the oven, so it is better to take it off the stove sooner than later.
9. Ladle a small amount of cream sauce in a casserole dish to cover bottom. Use a large enough casserole dish so that the cauliflower is a single layer.
10. Add the cauliflower and pour the remaining sauce over the cauliflower.
11. Sprinkle cheese over the top.
12. If adding bread crumbs, melt butter in a glass bowl in microwave and stir in bread crumbs. Sprinkle over top.
13. Bake for 5–15 minutes until the top is browned.
14. Remove from oven and sprinkle chopped chives over the top.

Lee Ping Quan's

EGGPLANT CROQUETTES
USS *MAYFLOWER* STYLE

*Makes 10–12 croquettes
(1 inch in diameter)*

INGREDIENTS

1–1½ pounds Italian eggplant (2 medium)
1 tablespoon salt
1 teaspoon pepper
1 tablespoon flour
1–2 tablespoons parmesan cheese
1 egg
1 tablespoon half-and-half
2 cups bread crumbs (if using panko, crumble with your hands into smaller pieces)
Vegetable oil for pan frying
Wax or parchment paper

This recipe is messy and sticky. The messiness can be reduced by keeping one hand "dry" and one hand "wet" when dipping the croquettes. The original recipe said to "shape like croquettes"—typically a cylinder, disk, or oval, like quenelles. We shaped the croquettes into disks, and this recipe makes 10–12 of them. These can be served with a sauce, such as tomato sauce, an aioli sauce, a spicy or lemon sauce, or ranch dressing. This recipe can be served as an appetizer at a dinner party (we recommend doubling the recipe) or as the vegetable dish for a weekend dinner for yourself.

The original recipe used bread crumbs. We chose panko bread crumbs because we like the texture and thought they would go well with the eggplant.

PREPARATION

1. Preheat oven to 375°F.
2. Place the eggplants onto a sheet pan and then into the oven for 40 minutes, until very soft. Remove and let cool.
3. Peel and mash up the eggplants, adding salt and pepper.
4. Add the flour and cheese, and mash/stir all together until combined. Cheese was not in the original recipe, but we wanted another binder that was not plain flour.
5. In a separate bowl, lightly whisk the egg and half-and-half.
6. In a separate bowl, have the panko ready.
7. Shape the eggplant mixture into a croquette or into the shape of your choice, dip it into the egg and cream mixture, and then dip it into the panko. Place the croquette on a plate covered with parchment paper Continue the same steps with the remaining eggplant mixture.
8. Place the plate with the finished croquettes in the refrigerator to firm up for approximately 30 minutes.
9. Heat a sauce pan with about ¼ inch of oil over medium heat. The oil is ready when it starts to shimmer. Or test a piece of panko in the oil. If it starts to sizzle, the oil is ready.
10. Gently drop each croquette into the oil—our pan fit about 6 at a time—until the bottoms start to brown, about 2 minutes. Then flip each croquette over (away from you) and fry for another minute or two. Both sides should be lightly browned.
11. Put each croquette on a plate covered with a paper towel. Repeat with the rest of the croquettes.
12. Serve each croquette with the sauce of your choice. We used homemade lemon aioli, but ranch dressing would be easier.

Lee Ping Quan's

FRIED GREEN ASPARAGUS TIPS

Serves 4–6 people

INGREDIENTS

1 large bunch of asparagus
1 teaspoon baking soda
Vegetable oil (canola, peanut, anything but olive)
3 eggs
1 tablespoon cream
1–2 cups stale bread crumbs (if store bought, unflavored, or panko, gently crumbled into smaller pieces)
Salt and pepper to taste

The original recipe called for boiling the asparagus for 25 minutes. We wondered whether the long boiling time was due to the varieties of asparagus back then being much tougher. Instead of an ice bath, which is a traditional culinary way of stopping cooking, rinsing under cold water works as well and is one less step.

PREPARATION

1. Wash asparagus and cut off the bottoms.
2. Drop tips into boiling water containing baking soda.
3. Boil for 3–5 minutes, until al dente, then immediately rinse under cold water to maintain green color.
4. Pat dry.
5. In a shallow saucepan, heat just enough oil to cover an asparagus tip lying flat. Start with medium heat. The oil is ready if it starts to ripple (or a bread crumb dropped in starts to bubble up).
6. In a shallow dish, beat eggs and cream together.
7. In a second shallow dish, season the bread crumbs with salt and pepper to your liking.
8. Dip each tip into the egg and cream mixture first, then the bread crumbs.
9. Fry in oil until lightly browned. Repeat each tip individually or try 2–3 at a time.
10. Set tips aside on a plate with a paper towel. Put the plate in an oven at 150°F to keep the tips warm while you finish the rest of the asparagus.
11. Serve as a side dish to a meal served for a special occasion.

Lee Ping Quan's

AVOCADO AND CITRUS SALAD WITH ENDIVE

Serves 8–12 people

VINAIGRETTE INGREDIENTS

1 shallot, finely diced
3 tablespoons rice wine vinegar
2 tablespoons reserved citrus juice (see below)
¼ cup olive oil
¼ cup canola (or other vegetable oil)
Salt and pepper to taste (approximately 1 teaspoon salt and ½ teaspoon black pepper)

SALAD INGREDIENTS

3 citrus fruits (oranges on the ripe side or ripe pink grapefruit), segmented, juice reserved
2 heads butter lettuce, leaves separated and washed, torn into large pieces
½ cup toasted nuts (almonds, pecans, or walnuts), chopped, or store-bought toasted and sweetened
2 heads endive, slivered
2 avocados, diced

The original name of this recipe was "Alligator Pears, Grapefruit and Oranges on Endive Salad." This combination of ingredients can still be found in modern salads.

We recommend using Cara Cara oranges or blood oranges instead of grapefruit. These are naturally sweeter. We have used sweet naval oranges as well.

Instead of dicing the citrus as Chef Quan recommended, segment the citrus into slices.

Endive is rarely served on its own as a salad. Especially with the abundance of lettuces, we recommend making your own mixed greens. We used butter lettuce and chopped the endive right before serving, so that is how the recipe is written.

Chef Quan's original recipe used a creamy dressing with mayonnaise. We decided to omit the creamy dressing and use a shallot–based vinaigrette to balance out the avocado and enhance the citrus.

VINAIGRETTE PREPARATION

1. Whisk the shallot with rice wine vinegar, the reserved citrus juice, and oils until slightly emulsified.
2. Add salt and pepper to taste.
3. Whisk in additional citrus juice to taste, about 2 tablespoons, but not so much as to make the dressing liquidy.

SALAD PREPARATION

1. To segment the citrus, use a very sharp knife, trim the ends off the citrus. Place on a cutting board and then trim the peel and pith lengthwise without removing any fruit. Hold the peeled citrus in your hand and slice lengthwise in between the membrane. The citrus becomes like a fan. Repeat with each segment.
2. Because endive and avocado both brown very quickly, prepare them right before serving.
3. Gently toss the salad ingredients with butter lettuce right before serving.
4. Use about 4–5 tablespoons of dressing for each head of lettuce and save the rest of the vinaigrette for another use.

STARTERS, SIDES, SALADS, AND SOUPS

Lee Ping Quan's

LEMON DRESSING
FOR SALAD AND SEAFOOD

Serves 8 people

INGREDIENTS

3 egg yolks
1 teaspoon mustard (nonspicy such as Dijon)
1 teaspoon salt
Juice of ½ lemon
1 pint oil (half olive, half canola)
Additional salt and pepper to taste (at least 1 tablespoon of salt and 1 teaspoon of ground black pepper)

Fresh vinaigrettes are always better than anything bottled. This dressing can be stored for 10 days. You can use this dressing for any salad green, as well as for a vegetable (either cooked or raw) plate. If making a kale salad, you can also dress the greens a couple of hours ahead of time.

We prefer to create dressings by hand, as opposed to using a food processor. In order to whisk by hand and add the olive oil at the same time, use a bowl that does not move while you are whisking, or roll a towel in a circle underneath the bowl to hold it in place.

Use a high-quality olive oil. If you find the taste of olive oil too strong, you can lighten it with canola oil, up to 50 percent for a less olivey taste. That is what we preferred. The result is like a hollandaise sauce, slightly more liquidy than an aioli.

Chef Quan also used this dressing for his fried shrimp recipe (see page 75).

PREPARATION

1. In a nonreactive bowl, whisk the egg yolks.
2. Add the mustard, salt, and lemon juice.
3. Whisk in the oil, a few droplets at a time, until the mixture starts to thicken. Then you can drizzle in the oil a bit more quickly.
4. Add salt and pepper.

Lee Ping Quan's
RUSSIAN DRESSING

Serves 8–12 people

INGREDIENTS

3 egg yolks
1 teaspoon mustard powder
1 teaspoon salt
1 pint oil
¼ cup sweet pickles, finely diced
1 small white onion, finely diced
1 clove garlic, finely chopped
Additional salt to taste
Black pepper (optional)

Originally we envisioned this to be like a Thousand Island dressing, pinkish in color. But it is not. The only difference between this dressing and the tartar dressing is the substitution of an onion for olives and the addition of garlic, as both this recipe and the tartar dressing use pickles and mustard.

Chef Quan's recipe does not specify what type of oil to use. We suggest using a good-quality vegetable oil, such as canola. You can even split it between a high-quality extra-virgin olive oil and canola.

Chef Quan did not add black pepper, but if you desire, you can add to taste at the end.

If you find raw garlic too strong, you can substitute 1 teaspoon garlic powder instead. Or you can gently sauté the garlic in olive oil, and, after cooling, add just the garlic to the dressing.

Serve with seafood.

PREPARATION

1. Beat the egg yolks and add them to the mustard powder and salt.
2. Slowly drizzle in the oil, while whisking to emulsify to a creamy dressing mixture. Whisk the oil with one hand and drizzle in the oil in a steady stream with the other hand (if possible) to a creamy dressing mixture.
3. Mix in the pickles, white onion, and garlic.
4. Add additional salt and black pepper to taste if desired.

Lee Ping Quan's
FRENCH DRESSING
FOR SALAD

Serves 8 people

INGREDIENTS

½ cup good-quality extra-virgin olive oil
2 tablespoons rice wine vinegar
1 tablespoon sugar
½ tablespoon chili sauce
½ teaspoon Worcestershire sauce
¼ teaspoon salt
¼ teaspoon ground black pepper

Chef Quan's recipe originally used two times as much vinegar as olive oil, making the dressing too sour and tart. We vastly reduced the vinegar and recommend using a softer vinegar like rice wine vinegar. Because we reduced the liquid components, we reduced the chili sauce as well.

This dressing can be used on any green salad.

PREPARATION

1. Whisk all the ingredients in a small bowl until well combined.

TARTAR DRESSING

Serves 8–12 people

INGREDIENTS

3 egg yolks
1 teaspoon mustard powder
1 teaspoon salt
1 pint oil
¼ cup sweet pickles, finely diced
1 small white onion, finely diced
1 dozen olives, finely chopped
Additional salt to taste
Black pepper (optional)

Chef Quan's version uses olives instead of capers. We suggest using green olives instead of Kalamata.

PREPARATION

1. Beat the egg yolks and then add to the mustard powder and salt.
2. Slowly drizzle in the oil, while whisking to emulsify to a creamy dressing mixture. Whisk the oil with one hand and drizzle in the oil in a steady stream with the other hand (if possible) to a creamy dressing mixture.
3. Mix in the pickles, white onion, and olives.
4. Add additional salt and black pepper to taste if desired.
5. Serve with baked or fried fish.

Lee Ping Quan's

CLAM CHOWDER
WHITE HOUSE STYLE

Serves 6–8 people

CHOWDER INGREDIENTS

2 tablespoons butter
¾ pound carrots (4 large), finely diced
¾ pound onions, finely diced
¾ pound celery (4 stalks), finely diced
1 quart fresh shucked clams (remove the black spot or substitute 5 cans of chopped clams, Bar Harbor or Snow are good brands), juice reserved
2 tablespoons flour
1–2 cups water
½ pint cream
2 pints milk (optional)
Pepper to taste
3 slices crusty white bread
Unsalted butter for frying

GARNISH

2 green peppers
4 pimientos (cherry red peppers) or any small sweet chili pepper
Unsalted butter for frying or sautéing

This soup is thinner than the very thick New England–style clam chowder.

The Gibralter-style option adds an interesting bitter note to the soup. We are not sure why Chef Quan deep fried the green peppers but sautéed the pimientos. We sautéed both.

This recipe can be used with oysters or white fish substituted for the clams. The original recipe called for Spanish mackerel, but a lighter-tasting white fish would also work.

We made significant changes to the cooking method of the original recipe. Chef Quan boiled the vegetables in 1 gallon of water until they were softened and then added the other ingredients to the vegetable broth. The resulting soup was extremely watery and unwieldy in volume. What worked better was to sauté the vegetables first, add the butter and flour, and then add water to thicken. Both milk and cream are not needed. You can omit the milk if you like, which is what we did. You do not need to substitute another liquid for the milk.

The original recipe used fresh shucked clams. We used canned clams.

The fried bread in butter gives this soup a decadent finish.

PREPARATION

1. In a Dutch oven, melt the butter and sauté the vegetables until softened, approximately 5 minutes.
2. Add the chopped clams and their juice.
3. Add the flour and, over medium heat, whisk until combined.
4. Add 1–2 cups of water, depending on your desired thickness, remembering that milk and cream will be added. Note that Chef Quan seemed to intend for the soup to be soupy as opposed to thick, so if you prefer a thicker soup, add less milk and cream.
5. Simmer for approximately 8 minutes to allow flavors to combine.
6. Whisk in the cream and milk and gently heat through.
7. Fry the bread in butter until it is crisp.
8. Sprinkle each portion of soup with small pieces of fried bread.
9. To make the chowder Gibraltar style, deep fry (or sauté) green peppers and pimientos. Chop up and combine. Then sprinkle 1 spoonful on each portion of soup.

Lee Ping Quan's

TOMATO CREAM SOUP
USS *MAYFLOWER* STYLE

Serves 4–8 people

INGREDIENTS

5 pounds red tomatoes, washed, destemmed (or canned peeled tomatoes)
2 tablespoons unsalted butter
2 tablespoons flour
1½ quarts unsalted beef or chicken stock (or vegetable if you want to keep soup vegetarian)
3 ounces tomato paste
1 tablespoon salt
1 teaspoon pepper
1 tablespoon sugar
1 teaspoon dried basil
1 teaspoon dried onion powder
1 teaspoon dried garlic powder
½ quart to 1 quart milk
½ quart cream
3 slices of white bread (we suggest baguette slices)
3 tablespoons unsalted butter
Fresh basil (optional)

Chef Quan's original recipe for cold tomato cream soup created a soup that was very pink in color. We preferred a darker red color to highlight the tomatoes, so we increased the amount of tomato product by adding a small can of tomato paste. You can also add an additional 2–3 pounds of tomatoes. Chef Quan also had a recipe for hot soup, but it included beef and egg (which we found odd), so we used the cold soup recipe and heated it. The end result was delicious. Just do not boil the end product as the cream will break.

We added sugar to balance out the acidity of the tomatoes. We also added dried basil, onion powder, and garlic powder for additional seasonings.

PREPARATION

1. To prepare fresh tomatoes, make a small "X" at the bottom of each tomato with a paring knife. Prepare a large bowl of ice water. Place tomatoes in boiling water for 30 seconds; then dip into the ice water. Remove skin. Blend the tomatoes in a blender or food processor.
2. In a Dutch oven or large pot, melt 2 tablespoons butter over medium heat.
3. Add flour and cook for 1 minute.
4. Whisk in beef or chicken stock.
5. Add the blended tomatoes, tomato paste, salt, pepper, sugar, basil, onion powder, and garlic powder.
6. Bring to a low boil, and boil down until combined and slightly thick.
7. If making a hot soup, add milk and cream and gently heat.
8. If making a cold soup, cool, and then add the milk and cream.
9. Sauté the baguette slices in a generous amount of butter.
10. To serve, ladle the soup into individual bowls with baguette slices over the top.
11. Optional: fresh basil can be soaked in the heated soup for a couple of minutes. The flavor of the basil will permeate the soup.

Lee Ping Quan's

CHICKEN NOODLE SOUP
WASHINGTON STYLE

Serves 8 people

STOCK INGREDIENTS

1 onion, diced
1 stalk celery, diced
1 carrot, diced
2 tablespoons olive oil
12 cups water
Full chicken breast (2 chicken breasts), bone-in, skin on or off (approximately 2 pounds)

SOUP INGREDIENTS

½ pound egg noodles
2 stalks celery, diced
2 carrots, diced
1 tablespoon salt
1 teaspoon pepper
1 teaspoon oregano
1 teaspoon dried basil
Shredded chicken (see above and steps 2–5)

Instead of using chicken broth, which is easily purchased in a supermarket today, we wanted a homemade broth similar to Chef Quan's. We used a full chicken breast, which was much easier to handle than boiling an entire chicken. Chef Quan also added beef or pork bones, so if you have extra carcasses from a roast chicken, you can add them to the stock.

PREPARATION

1. In a large soup pot, sauté the vegetables for the stock in the olive oil until softened.
2. Add water and then the chicken breast.
3. Bring to a boil and simmer for 45 minutes.
4. Remove chicken and cool slightly.
5. Remove the skin and shred the chicken.
6. Strain the vegetables out of the broth and discard. There should be approximately 8 cups of liquid left.
7. Put the broth back into the soup pot. Bring back to a boil and add the egg noodles, fresh celery and carrots, and seasonings.
8. When the egg noodles are almost done, add the shredded chicken back in.
9. If you would like more broth, add 1–2 cups more water.

Lee Ping Quan's

CHICKEN AND RICE PORRIDGE

Serves 6–8 people

INGREDIENTS

1 carcass of a roast chicken or turkey (or one whole chicken)
1 cup rice

CONDIMENTS

Green onion, sliced
Peanuts, chopped, roasted, and salted
Soy sauce to taste

Chef Quan's original recipe was entitled "Chicken Broth for Convalescents," implying that it was a clear broth. However, using rice resulted in a thicker porridge, which reminded us more of the traditional Chinese porridge. Instead of crackers, we suggest serving the porridge with green onion, chopped peanuts, and soy sauce.

Ideally, a leftover carcass of a roast chicken or turkey works. But you can start with a whole chicken like Chef Quan did.

PREPARATION

1. Simmer the carcass or whole chicken and rice in enough water to cover until rice thickens, approximately 2 hours.
2. Remove the chicken and shred it, and add back some of the shredded chicken if desired.
3. Serve in soup bowls and top with the condiments.

Entrées

Lee Ping Quan's

FILET MIGNON
PRESIDENT HARDING'S DISH

Serves 8–10 people

INGREDIENTS

½ cup sherry
Juice of 1 lemon
1 tablespoon Worcestershire sauce
4 pounds filet, each filet 6–8 ounces
Salt and pepper
8 slices bacon (one for each filet)
1 teaspoon butter for each filet
1½ pounds fresh mushrooms, sliced
2 tablespoons butter
2 tablespoons flour
1½–2 cups beef or chicken stock
1½ teaspoons sherry

Chef Quan's recipe placed the bacon on top of the filet and then broiled the entire filet in the oven for the entire cooking time. We have provided an alternative cooking method that suited our kitchen.

PREPARATION

1. Preheat oven to 500°F.
2. Combine sherry, lemon juice, and Worcestershire sauce. The original recipe did not specify portions, so these are our suggestions, but you can adjust the ratios to your liking.
3. Dip each filet in the mixture, set aside, and then season with salt and pepper.
4. Place a long slice of bacon across the top of each filet and stick toothpicks into it to hold it in place.
5. Roast at 500°F for 8–11 minutes, and then turn on the broiler and broil for 3 minutes.
6. Rest the filets in the oven for 5 minutes, until the internal temperature reduces to 120°F.
7. Put a pat of butter on each filet.
8. In a large saucepan, sauté mushrooms in butter over medium heat.
9. Add flour and sauté until combined. Add stock to desired thickness.
10. Add 1½ teaspoons sherry. Pour mushroom sauce over each filet.

ALTERNATIVE PREPARATION

Tie each piece of bacon around the side of the filet and secure with a toothpick. In an oven-proof pan (with 1 teaspoon of oil), sear each side of the filet until dark brown over medium-high–high heat. Rest in a 450–500°F oven for 8 minutes, until the internal temperature reduces to 120°F. As the meat is resting, the mushrooms can be sautéed in the same pan as the filet was seared in. Finish sauce as above.

Lee Ping Quan's

PRESIDENT COOLIDGE'S RICE AND CURRY
WITH CONDIMENTS

Serves 4 people

INGREDIENTS

1 pound lean ground veal (or ½ pound veal and ½ pound pork)
1 egg
2 shallots, minced
½ tablespoon cumin
½ tablespoon coriander
1 tablespoon salt
¼ teaspoon black pepper
2½ tablespoons butter
1–2 tablespoons curry powder of your choice (we used McCormick's)
2 tablespoons flour
2–3 cups to 1 quart unsalted chicken or beef stock
2 tablespoons cream

CONDIMENTS FOR SERVING

Chopped fine—½ cup each of as many or as few as you like:

Cucumbers, tomatoes, celery, green peppers, green olives, sweet pickles, raw onion (or shallots), fried onion (or fried shallots), bacon, hard-boiled egg, almonds, shredded unsweetened coconut, ham, cheddar cheese, chutney (your choice of flavor, can be store bought), cooked white fish (sardines or tuna or anchovies would work), currants (the original recipe called for fried, but unfried would work well).

We are curious as to the origin of this recipe and when President Coolidge was introduced to curry, since his only travel outside the United States was to Cuba.

This is a recipes for meatballs, so curry meatballs would be a more appropriate title. The unusual condiments are what makes this recipe unique. The original recipe included "Bombay duck" as a condiment. Because we discovered that Bombay duck is not a duck, but a fish in Bombay, we included anchovies or sardines as an optional condiment.

You can mix and match as many or as few of the condiments as you like. We never used all of the condiments at once. We chose easy combinations such as a mix of cucumbers and tomatoes with the meatballs, but other combinations such as olives and pickles would work, too.

The original recipe included curry powder in the instructions, but not in the list of ingredients, so we do not know how much. For the home cook, a store-bought yellow curry powder works.

For the meatballs, we tested both veal and a combination of half veal and half pork. The veal was more buttery in texture, but both were delicious. We wanted to add some additional flavor to the meatballs, so we included shallots and some spices.

PREPARATION

1. Preheat oven to 400°F.
2. Combine meat, egg, shallots, cumin, and coriander, and then season with salt and pepper.
3. Roll in small (½ inch) balls and bake for 10 minutes. Set aside.
4. In a frying pan, combine the butter, curry powder, and flour, and mix together until lightly browned.
5. Whisk in the stock until thickened to the consistency you desire. We used about 2–3 cups.
6. Drop the meatballs into this mixture, cooking for an additional 2–3 minutes.
7. Complete by adding the cream and lightly stirring all together.
8. Pour curry over white rice, and serve with condiments.

Lee Ping Quan's
STEAMED BONELESS FISH

Serves 4 people

INGREDIENTS

1–1½ pounds white fish filets (sea bass, tilapia, snapper, rockfish, halibut, and cod are all good choices)
1 cup vegetable oil
2 tablespoons Chinese rice wine
4 cloves garlic, minced
½ cup soy sauce
2 tablespoons chili sauce or chili oil
4 green onions for garnish, sliced or julienned thin

Chef Quan originally had a recipe for steamed boneless chicken in the Chinese Dishes section of his cookbook. Steaming an entire chicken or even chicken parts could prove challenging for a home cook, so we adapted this recipe to use fish filets instead of chicken. We adapted the condiments to suit fish instead of chicken.

PREPARATION

1. Steam white fish filets for approximately 8 minutes by whatever method chosen. We set up a steamer by placing the fish filets on a rack or in a bowl. We placed the rack or bowl in a large pot or wok that has 2 inches of water in it. Make sure the water does not touch the fish filets.
2. Cover the pot and steam for 8 minutes.
3. Place fish on a serving platter.
4. In a separate pan, heat oil until sizzling.
5. Add rice wine (it might flame!), then garlic and soy sauce. Stir in chili sauce.
6. Pour mixture over fish.
7. Add green onions as a garnish.
8. Serve with white rice, scooping plenty of sauce over rice.

Lee Ping Quan's
WHITE HOUSE FRIED CHICKEN

Serves 6–8 people

CHICKEN INGREDIENTS

1 cut-up whole chicken deboned or boned and skin on or off (or 4½ pounds of chicken parts your choice, deboned and skinless)

Salt and pepper

1–2 tablespoons sherry

Frying oil such as peanut, corn, or canola

1 cup flour

3 eggs

1 tablespoon cream

1½–2 cups unflavored bread crumbs, or crumbled panko crumbs

SAUCE INGREDIENTS

1½ pounds mushrooms, button or brown

2½ tablespoons flour

2½ tablespoons butter

2 cups chicken stock

½ cup heavy cream

2 tablespoons sherry

This is a fork-and-knife fried chicken, served with a mushroom sauce. The cooking times will differ vastly depending on whether the bone is in or not. If you decide to keep the chicken bone in, increase the cooking time until the chicken has a 160°F internal temperature; that could be up to 15 minutes for chicken thighs. The original recipe called for deboning, which makes the chicken cook faster, so that is what we did. You can experiment with coatings. We sprinkled paprika in addition to salt and pepper. You can also add dried herbs such as oregano, parsley, and basil.

The smaller the chicken pieces, the easier they are to fry. Huge breast pieces should be cut in two. Boneless skin-on thighs and breasts are ideal. We cut the breasts in half and used the tenders. Bone-in, skin-on wings, drumettes, or chicken legs can also be used. This recipe has been rewritten for pan-frying. A deep fryer can work as well.

The original recipe served the chicken with "potato croquettes and buttered celery." Modern equivalents would be mashed potatoes and coleslaw.

PREPARATION

1. Sprinkle chicken parts with salt and pepper and drizzle with sherry.
2. Heat a shallow frying pan with 1–2 inches of oil until oil has ripples and/or, when you drop bread crumbs in the oil, it bubbles slightly.
3. Set up three shallow bowls (or pie plates)—one with the flour, one with the eggs that have been beaten with the cream, and one with bread crumbs. Dip each piece of chicken in the flour, then the egg-cream mixture, and then the bread crumbs.
4. Pan fry each piece for approximately 6–8 minutes, turning each side for even cooking and browning. Oil will bubble around the pieces of chicken. Turn down the heat to low to prevent dark browning on the outside. Chicken is cooked through at 160°F. We took out the chicken when the internal temperature reached 140°F and allowed the chicken to rest to 160°F. If you have a deep fryer, heat the fryer to 350°F and drop each piece of chicken into fryer. When the piece of chicken bubbles and rises to the top, it is done.
5. Set the chicken aside on brown paper bags or paper towels. Keep the chicken warm in a 150°F oven.
6. In a separate saucepan, make the mushroom sauce. Sauté the mushrooms until brown. Add the flour and butter and brown.
7. Add chicken stock, heavy cream, and sherry, whisking until creamy.
8. Pour mushroom sauce on chicken.

Lee Ping Quan's

BARBECUE SADDLE OF LAMB
WITH OYSTER DRESSING

Serves 6–8 people

OYSTER DRESSING INGREDIENTS

- 8–10 cups of homemade croutons, made from fresh white bread
- ¼ cup olive oil
- 1 tablespoon salt
- 1 teaspoon pepper
- 2 medium onions (or 1 large onion), diced
- 1 cup celery, diced
- 1–2 tablespoons oil for sautéing
- 8 ounces mushrooms, sliced
- 1 knob butter
- 1 teaspoon sage
- 1 or 2 8-ounce cans of oysters, chopped, liquid reserved
- 2 eggs, beaten
- Salt and pepper to taste

LAMB INGREDIENTS

- 1 boneless leg of lamb (about 5 pounds)
- 15 cloves garlic
- 5 tablespoons rosemary
- Approximately 2 tablespoons salt
- Approximately 1 teaspoon ground pepper
- 1 tablespoon sherry

This recipe can be used for any large cut of lamb such as boneless leg of lamb, rack of lamb, or lamb loin. Just select a large cut to roast and catch the juices. Chef Quan used lamb loin. We like boneless leg of lamb, for its fat, flavor, and availability, so that is what we used.

Chef Quan did not have any seasonings other than salt, pepper, and sherry. We included a paste of chopped rosemary and garlic, combined with Chef Quan's original recipe, to be stuffed inside the lamb leg. For a large loin or a boneless leg of lamb, roll and tie the lamb. But you can also choose to not roll the lamb, as in Chef Quan's original recipe. This makes the recipe much easier, and the cooking time is vastly reduced, to approximately 30 minutes. If your leg of lamb is too long for the roasting pan, you can cut it in half.

Chef Quan's original recipe contemplated hanging saddles of lamb on a barbecue iron. We chose to roast to catch the juices for the oyster dressing.

We grilled the lamb as well. The only disadvantage is that there are no juices.

We used Chef Quan's signature addition of sherry as the acid, but lemon juice and zest can be used as well or instead.

Chef Quan did not marinate the meat overnight. But you can, by rubbing the paste over the lamb and then refrigerating it overnight in a bowl or a Ziploc bag.

We typically associate oyster dressing with Thanksgiving and turkey. Whatever lamb cut and cooking method you use, we strongly suggest serving it with the oyster dressing, as Chef Quan did. This combination was delicious and a pleasant surprise.

Oysters are an acquired taste, so we reduced the oysters to one 8-ounce can and added 8 ounces of mushrooms. Because the lamb is so flavorful, two 8-ounce cans of oysters can be added. Chef Quan's original recipe called for a quart, which we do not recommend unless you really like oysters.

We suggest making croutons and processing them slightly in a food processor. Store-bought bread crumbs can also be used.

OYSTER DRESSING PREPARATION

1. Cut the loaf of bread into pieces.
2. Toss in olive oil, salt, and pepper.
3. Bake in a 350°F oven until browned, approximately 12 minutes. Let cool slightly.
4. Process in a food processor until mostly crumbs. You will have a mixture of crumbs and chunks. Set aside.
5. Sauté the onions and celery in 1–2 tablespoons of oil until softened.
6. Add mushrooms until softened.
7. Add the knob of butter.
8. Add the sage and oysters and sauté all together for 2–3 minutes.
9. In a large bowl, combine croutons, oyster mixture, and oyster juice.
10. Add the eggs. The entire mixture should be moistened. If it is not, add stock to moisten. Salt and pepper to taste. Keep in mind that the lamb juice and fat from the roasting pan will be added to this so do not oversalt.
11. Transfer to a 2 or 3 quart casserole dish.
12. Bake in a 325°F oven for approximately 30 minutes until lightly browned.

LAMB PREPARATION

1. Increase the oven temperature to 400°F.
2. Prepare the lamb by removing large layers of fat.
3. Prepare a roasting pan by adding 1–2 cups of water to just below the roasting rack. Make sure the water does not touch the meat. Place excess fat on the roasting rack if you desire.
4. Process the garlic, rosemary, salt, pepper, and sherry into a paste. Add more sherry to make it a liquidy paste.
5. Rub the paste over the insides of the lamb if you roll it. Roll and then season the exterior of the roll. If you are not rolling it, season the entire lamb at once. Place the lamb on a rack in the roasting pan.
6. For a flat lamb, roast for 25–35 minutes until the internal temperature at the thickest part reads 120°F.
7. Remove the lamb from the oven and let it rest until the internal temperature is 130°F, for 5–10 minutes. For a rolled lamb, roast for 15 minutes at 400°F. Turn heat down to 300°F and roast for an additional 45–60 minutes, checking temperature at 45 minutes at thickest part, until temperature is 120°F. Remove the lamb from the oven and let it rest until the internal temperature is 130°F. Cover with an aluminum foil tent.
8. Pour the lamb juices in the roasting pan over the oyster dressing. Slice and serve lamb over dressing.

Lee Ping Quan's

MRS. COOLIDGE'S FAVORITE CHOP SUEY

Serves 4–6 people

INGREDIENTS

8-ounce can water chestnuts

8-ounce can bamboo shoots

1 bunch of celery hearts

¾ pound Chinese greens (we used baby bok choy, but spinach also works)

4–6 ounces Chinese beans (we used fava, but green beans or bean sprouts are good alternatives)

1 pound white meat chicken

¼ cup unsalted butter (or less, if desired)

¼ cup cut vegetable oil (or less, if desired)

2–3 cups chicken stock (homemade, boxed, or canned)

Salt and pepper

1 tablespoon cornstarch

2 tablespoons soy sauce

1½ tablespoons Chinese rice wine (or sherry)

Chef Quan's original recipe referred to "Chinese beans." We used fresh fava beans, which added 30 minutes of cooking time. Quan could have meant Chinese bean sprouts, which are easier and more commonly seen today.

Quan's original recipe used only butter. We changed this to half butter and half vegetable oil to increase the burning point, and butter in a Chinese recipe is unusual. We kept this combination for the variations as we were not sure whether Quan accidentally omitted the butter from the protein variations other than chicken, and we thought butter went well with the other proteins, particularly the seafood.

The convenience of this recipe is that any vegetables can be used—broccoli, peppers, green beans—that you have left over in your refrigerator. Or, if you are like us and do not particularly care for water chestnuts or bamboo shoots, substitutions are easily available. You can also skip an ingredient and the amounts of each ingredient are forgiving in the sense that nothing has to be exact in a stir fry. We like the cooking method of sautéing everything separately so it is not one big mush of sloppy vegetables. The cornstarch-based slurry, which gradually thickens as you pour it over everything, creates a nice sauce to be eaten with the rice.

PREPARATION

1. Julienne water chestnuts, bamboo shoots, hearts of celery, bottoms of Chinese greens (if there are any), Chinese beans (unless using fava beans), and chicken. If using fava beans, take out of the pod, blanch in boiling water for 1 minute, cool under cold water, and then peel.
2. Using a 3-quart saucepan or wok, stir fry the chicken and the vegetables separately in a combination of half butter and half oil until lightly tender (approximately 3 minutes each).
3. Place the vegetables and chicken together back in the wok and pour the chicken stock over it.
4. Boil for 5 minutes and season with salt and pepper.
5. In a separate bowl, create a slurry with cornstarch, soy sauce, and Chinese rice wine.
6. Add to the mixture and boil for an additional 3–7 minutes, until chicken is cooked through. Try to not overcook the vegetables: you will know if the vegetables (in our case, the bok choy) start losing their bright green color.
7. Serve with white rice.

VARIATIONS

Pork Chop Suey: Substitute 1 pound white meat pork, julienned, for chicken. Add 1 bunch of green onions, chopped, with the vegetables.

Shrimp Chop Suey: Substitute 1 pound fresh shrimp, diced, for chicken. Add 1 bunch of green onions, chopped, with the vegetables.

Lobster Chop Suey: Substitute 1 pound lobster meat, diced, for chicken.

Scallop Chop Suey: Substitute 1 pound scallops, diced, for chicken. Add 1 bunch of green onions, chopped, with the vegetables.

Lee Ping Quan's

CHICKEN CHOW MEIN

MRS. COOLIDGE'S FAVORITE DISH

Serves 4–6 people

INGREDIENTS

1 tablespoon cornstarch

2 tablespoons dark soy sauce

1½ tablespoons Chinese rice wine (or sherry or mirin)

1½ pounds boneless chicken breast and/or thighs, diced into small pieces

2 stalks green onion, sliced

2 tablespoons oil for sautéing

2 stalks celery

4 ounces bean sprouts

1 cup fresh bamboo shoots, sliced

Vegetables to your liking, such as bok choy, peppers (red, green, or orange), Napa cabbage, mushrooms, tomatoes, even long green beans (cut shorter) or broccoli; we prefer Napa cabbage

Approximately ½ cup water, depending on type of noodle

About 1 pound noodles of your choice

This recipe can be modernized by using colorful fresh vegetables instead of water chestnuts and bamboo shoots, boneless chicken already prepared at the market, and packaged noodles. Using more fresh vegetables turns the dish into more of a "subgum"—a Chinese mixture of meats and vegetables—and looks more like the chow mein we see in Chinese restaurants today.

Our favorite vegetable to use in chow mein is Napa cabbage, because it melts into the noodles. Do not go overboard on vegetables because chow mein is about the noodles and the sauce. If you can find them, use fresh bamboo shoots. Their flavor is so strong it will permeate the dish with a fresh taste. We found ours at May Wah, a Chinese market on Clement Street in San Francisco, and using them brought us joy when we tasted them in the noodles.

Chef Quan had a recipe for fried noodles, made by hand. Because of the abundance of noodles in modern times, we recommend using store-bought noodles. The use of deep fried noodles reminds me of the La Choy canned noodles, and a Cantonese restaurant near me pours the chicken mixture over deep fried noodles. We prefer to use a nonfried soft egg noodle or dried noodle. Spaghetti noodles are the easiest. If you live near an Asian market, a fresh sturdy egg noodle would work, too. We used a brand of precooked egg noodles called "Hon's" Asian Comfort Food Chow Mein Noodles. The only type of noodle to avoid is the thin and soft wheat noodles, as those are better for soup, as opposed to a stir fry. Instead of pouring the mixture over the noodles, we prefer to stir everything together.

What does stay the same, however, is the original sauce ingredients. Either a dark or regular soy sauce works. We chose to use dark as we preferred the color.

Protein substitutions can be made. Chef Quan included a recipe for duck chow mein (see page 108), but, like the chop sueys, shrimp, lean pork, and lobster can be used.

PREPARATION

1. In a separate small bowl, combine cornstarch, soy sauce, and rice wine.
2. In a large saucepan or wok, heat oil and sauté chicken with onion until chicken is cooked through, approximately 8 minutes.
3. Add all the vegetables to the chicken and cook over medium heat, until the vegetables are softened. Add cabbage and bok choy last as they take the least amount of time to cook.
4. Pour the cornstarch mixture over the chicken until the sauce is thickened. We added ½ cup water for more sauce. The amount of water needed will depend on the type of noodle you use. For our precooked noodle, ½ cup of water was just enough.
5. Meanwhile, prepare noodles in accordance with the package instructions (or add the precooked noodles directly to pan). If you choose to use the block of flash-fried dried noodles, soften them in boiling water first and then set aside.
6. In a large bowl, mix the noodles and the chicken mixture together. You can do this in your saucepan or wok with the heat turned off if there is enough room.

Lee Ping Quan's
DUCK CHOW MEIN, À LA QUAN

Serves 6–8 people

INGREDIENTS

1 tablespoon cornstarch

2 tablespoons dark soy sauce

1½ tablespoons Chinese rice wine (or sherry or mirin)

2 stalks green onion, sliced

2 stalks celery

2 tablespoons oil for sautéing

½ head of medium-size Napa cabbage

½–1 package bean sprouts

1 cup fresh bamboo shoots, sliced

1 roast Chinese duck, shredded, bones removed, include skin, juice saved

Approximately ½ cup water, depending on type of noodle

About 1 pound noodles of your choice

Salt and pepper to taste

Chef Quan's original recipe called for "boiling a duck for 45 minutes over a low fire." Thankfully, roast Chinese ducks can be purchased in a Chinese market. Look for them hanging in a window. Buy a whole duck, and ask that it be cut up. Mine always comes with juice. Be sure to save that.

PREPARATION

1. In a separate small bowl, combine cornstarch, soy sauce, and rice wine.
2. In a large saucepan or a wok, sauté green onion and celery in the oil over medium-high heat.
3. Add cabbage, bean sprouts, and bamboo shoots and sauté until slightly softened.
4. Add duck and stir for 1 minute.
5. Pour the cornstarch mixture over the duck until the sauce is thickened, add ½ cup water. The amount of water needed will depend on the type of noodle you use. We used precooked noodles, and ½ cup was enough. However, more may be needed, up to 1 cup.
6. Add reserved duck juice.
7. Meanwhile, prepare noodles in accordance with the package instructions (or add the precooked noodles directly to the pan).
8. Add noodles to the saucepan and stir to combine, then serve.

Lee Ping Quan's

TRICOLOR PEPPER STEAK

Serves 4–6 people

INGREDIENTS

- 1½ pounds steak (rib-eye, tri-tip, or sirloin)
- 3 peppers (green, yellow, or red, or a combination), julienned
- 1 5–10 ounce package mushrooms, any type such as button, crimini, shiitake, sliced
- 2 tomatoes, diced
- 1 tablespoon cornstarch
- 1 tablespoon soy sauce
- 1 tablespoon Chinese rice wine
- 2 tablespoons vegetable oil (canola, peanut, not olive) for stir frying

The three different colors of the dish originally as written were brown (beef), green (peppers), and red (tomatoes), but with the availability of red, yellow, and orange peppers, this dish can be even more attractive visually with up to six colors. The original recipe was entitled "Three Different Color Peppered Steak" and called for cutting the steak and tomatoes into "diamond-shaped" pieces. Instead, we recommend simply dicing and slicing. Initially, we found tomatoes an odd addition to a stir fry, but they add a sweetness and texture for a nice balance. We resisted the urge to marinate the meat, although many recipes call for a marinade today. Instead, rely on good cuts of meat and do not overcook.

The original recipe used chestnut starch. Cornstarch is a more common modern-day alternative.

Sherry, which Chef Quan uses heavily throughout his cookbook, is a good substitute if you do not have access to Chinese rice wine. Shaoxing rice wine is the type I use. You can also use mirin, the Japanese cooking wine, if you have it, but it is sweeter than Chinese rice wine.

PREPARATION

1. Cut up all the ingredients. Slice the steak into thin slices. You can freeze the steak slightly to make it easier to slice.
2. In a small bowl, combine cornstarch, soy sauce, and rice wine.
3. Heat wok or a large saucepan over high heat. Add oil.
4. Add steak, and sear for 3 minutes. Resist the urge to continually touch the beef as you need to allow the meat to sear.
5. Reduce heat to medium. Add mushrooms and fry for 2–3 minutes, stirring occasionally.
6. Add peppers and fry for 3 minutes until slightly softened.
7. Add tomatoes and fry for 1–2 minutes.
8. Pour in the cornstarch mixture. The stir fry is done when the sauce is thickened. If you need to add water to thin out the sauce to your liking, drizzle a couple of tablespoons in slowly.
9. Serve with white rice.

Baked Goods and Desserts

Lee Ping Quan's
ALMOND COOKIES
PRESIDENT HARDING'S FAVORITE

Makes 16–18 1-inch cookies

INGREDIENTS

1 egg white, room temperature
½ cup powdered sugar
½ cup unsalted butter, softened
1 teaspoon vanilla
1½ cups pastry flour
Up to ⅓ cup milk (any fat level)
Sliced almonds

These cookies are not like the Chinese almond cookies you see at the store or have at Chinese restaurants. Instead, these are slightly dense mini vanilla cakes that are not very sweet. They taste like vanilla scones.

The original recipe called for "1 large spoon milk." We used ⅓ cup, but any amount up to that can be used to moisten the batter. We translated Chef Quan's direction of "moderate oven" to 325°F and baked the cookies for 10 minutes, instead of the original 30 minutes.

PREPARATION

1. Preheat oven to 325°F.
2. Beat egg white until stiff and place in the refrigerator.
3. In a mixer, beat together powdered sugar and butter until fluffy.
4. Add vanilla.
5. Add flour and mix until combined, adding in milk to moisten.
6. Gently fold in egg whites until combined.
7. The batter does not spread so whatever shape the batter is before baking will generally be what the baked cookie will look like. So you can roll and pat down into small disks, drop spoonfuls, or pipe onto a greased cookie sheet or Silpat, a silicone baking mat. Place a sliced almond in the middle of each cookie.
8. Bake for 8–12 minutes until very lightly browned, rotating halfway through.

Lee Ping Quan's
OATMEAL COOKIES
USS *MAYFLOWER* STYLE

Makes 24 large cookies

INGREDIENTS

½ pound flour
1 teaspoon baking powder
1½ teaspoons cinnamon
½ teaspoon salt
1½ cups sugar
½ pound butter, room temperature
3 egg yolks
1½ teaspoons vanilla
3 egg whites, room temperature
½ pound quick cooking oats

Like many of Chef Quan's cookie recipes, these cookies flatten out—given the butter-to-flour ratio—even with the addition of baking powder. We are fortunate to have quick-cooking oats and so do not need to dry out the oats, as Chef Quan did.

PREPARATION

1. Preheat oven to 300°F.
2. Prepare greased cookie sheets, nonstick baking pans, or parchment paper on baking sheets.
3. Combine flour, baking powder, cinnamon, and salt. Set aside.
4. In a stand mixer, cream the sugar with the butter until fluffy.
5. Add yolks one at a time, then vanilla extract.
6. Slowly add in the flour mixture.
7. Move this batter to a large bowl with a wide bottom.
8. In a separate bowl, beat egg whites until stiff.
9. Gently fold egg whites into the batter in a large bowl using as few strokes to combine as possible.
10. Gently fold in oats.
11. Scoop 1 tablespoon of batter for each cookie onto the cookie sheets. These cookies spread out so make sure there is plenty of room in between the cookies.
12. Bake for 20 minutes, checking after 10 minutes to rotate.

Lee Ping Quan's
PEANUT COOKIES
USS *MAYFLOWER* STYLE

Makes 48 cookies

INGREDIENTS

¾ pound granulated sugar
1½ cups water
3 egg whites, room temperature
1 pinch salt
Juice of 1 lemon
½ pound unsalted peanuts, finely chopped
½ cup powdered sugar

These cookies were like nothing we had seen before: they are meringue-like cookies, as opposed to peanut-butter-drop cookies. Even though there are multiple cooking methods that require many different types of cooking equipment, we found them easy to make. Like meringues, they are very sweet, but the peanuts balance out the sweetness.

PREPARATION

1. Preheat oven to 300°F.
2. Combine sugar and water and boil until a candy thermometer reads 240°F (what professional bakers call "soft-ball stage"), approximately 10–12 minutes. The sugar bubbles will gradually increase in size. The sugar mixture may turn a little light brown depending on the type of sugar you use, but do not let the sugar caramelize.
3. Meanwhile, in a stand mixer, beat the egg whites until stiff. Once stiff, turn the stand mixer down to low to keep the egg whites moving, until the sugar is ready.
4. With the stand mixer on low, slowly pour the hot mixture into the bowl, pouring along the side of the bowl to avoid splashing, until the texture is thick and creamy.
5. Add a pinch of salt.
6. Add the lemon juice.
7. Add the peanuts.
8. Add the powdered sugar, slowly.
9. Pipe cookies into small circle shapes on a buttered cookie sheet sprinkled with a little flour (or parchment paper). Bake for 5 minutes.
10. Option: spread icing in between two cookies to make a sandwich. Homemade icing or any store-bought icing can be used as needed.

Lee Ping Quan's
CHOCOLATE COOKIES
CHOCOLATE CHIP

Makes 36–42 large cookies

INGREDIENTS

½ pound flour
⅓ cup unsweetened high-quality cocoa powder
1 teaspoon baking powder
½ teaspoon salt
1½ cups sugar
½ pound butter, room temperature
3 egg yolks
¼ cup semisweet chocolate chips, melted
1½ teaspoons vanilla extract
3 egg whites, room temperature
1¾ cup semisweet chocolate chips

We added chocolate chips and cocoa powder to Chef Quan's original recipe, and reduced the butter, to increase the deep chocolate taste. These make great cookies for ice cream sandwiches as well. The chocolate chips can be melted in the microwave or over a double boiler. Either way, just make sure the chocolate is not heated too quickly and stir frequently. We used low heat or microwave for 15 seconds at a time.

PREPARATION

1. Preheat oven to 300°F.
2. Prepare greased cookie sheets, nonstick baking pans, or parchment paper on baking sheets.
3. Combine flour, cocoa powder, baking powder, and salt.
4. In a stand mixer, cream the sugar with the butter until fluffy.
5. Add the egg yolks one at a time.
6. Slowly add in the flour mixture.
7. Add the melted chocolate then the vanilla extract. Move this batter to a large bowl with a wide bottom.
8. In a separate bowl, beat the egg whites until stiff.
9. Gently fold the egg whites into the batter.
10. Gently fold in the chocolate chips.
11. Scoop 1 tablespoon of batter for each cookie onto the cookie sheets. Make sure there is plenty of space between the cookies as they spread very wide.
12. Bake for 10 minutes, checking after 6–7 minutes to rotate.

Lee Ping Quan's
VANILLA ALMOND COOKIES
POTOMAC STYLE

Approximately 24 cookies

INGREDIENTS

½ pound flour
1 teaspoon baking powder
½ teaspoon salt
1½ cups sugar
½ pound butter, room temperature
3 egg yolks
1½ teaspoons vanilla extract
3 egg whites, room temperature
½ pound chopped almonds

Whenever we see the words "almond cookies," we automatically think of the modern Chinese almond cookies. But these cookies are entirely different. They are paper thin, owing to the very little flour in the recipe. We suggest rolling them into tuiles or forming them into different shapes and serving them with tea.

PREPARATION

1. Preheat oven to 300°F.
2. Prepare greased cookie sheets, nonstick baking pans, or parchment paper on baking sheets.
3. Combine flour, baking powder, and salt.
4. In a stand mixer, cream the sugar with the butter until fluffy.
5. Add the egg yolks one at a time.
6. Slowly add in the flour mixture, then the vanilla extract. Move this batter to a large bowl with a wide bottom.
7. In a separate bowl, beat the egg whites until stiff.
8. Gently fold the egg whites into the batter.
9. Once combined, gently fold in the almonds.
10. Scoop 1 tablespoon of batter for each cookie.
11. Bake for 10–15 minutes, checking after 6–7 minutes to rotate.
12. You can leave the cookies flat as wide circles, or, when still warm, roll them into tuiles (cigar shapes).

Lee Ping Quan's

STRAWBERRY SHORTCAKE
USS *MAYFLOWER* STYLE

Serves 6–8 people

CAKE INGREDIENTS

6 eggs
2 ounces granulated sugar
2 tablespoons cream (we used whipping cream)
1 teaspoon vanilla
3 ounces unbleached all-purpose flour
½ tablespoon baking powder

STRAWBERRY FILLING INGREDIENTS

1 quart strawberries, halved, saving some whole for top layer to decorate
2–3 tablespoons sugar

WHIPPED CREAM INGREDIENTS

1 tablespoon mascarpone cheese or cream cheese
4 tablespoons powdered sugar
1 quart whipping cream

The cake is slightly dense, eggy and spongy, and very sweet. We tested a couple of versions, including one that increased the amount of cream because the original recipe contained a lot of sugar but no butter. The result was a flat and overly sweet cake, so we decided to reduce the amount of sugar by half. The original recipe did not rely on rising agents so what is poured in the cake pan is exactly what it looks like after baking. For insurance, we added baking powder so that it does rise a bit. Use standard 8- or 9-inch cake pans. We halved the recipe, as a four-layer cake using 12 eggs can be unwieldy to make at home.

The original recipe specified beating the eggs and sugar together "until thick." We used a stand mixer with a whisk attachment and whisked on high for 5 minutes, in order to aerate the batter. Then we turned the power way down and gently mixed in the flour. We used sifted unbleached flour but pastry or cake flour can also be used. Sifting the flour does matter, so do not skip this step. We switched the order as well, adding the cream and vanilla before the flour.

PREPARATION

1. Preheat the oven to 300°F.
2. Prepare two greased or sprayed cake pans with parchment paper.
3. In a stand mixer with the whisk attachment, whisk eggs and sugar together for 5 minutes on high.
4. Turn power down and add cream and vanilla.
5. Sift flour and baking powder together and slowly add to egg and sugar mixture until fully incorporated.
6. Pour batter into the cake pans.
7. Bake for 25 minutes (check after 20 minutes).
8. Cool and remove from cake pans. You will need a knife along the edges.
9. For the filling, toss strawberries with sugar.
10. For the whipped cream, whip cheese and powdered sugar in a stand mixer until combined. Add cream until soft peaks form. Reserve two cups of whipped cream for the top layer.
11. Layer strawberries and whipped cream between the two cake layers.
12. Decorate the top layer with whole strawberries and remaining whipped cream.

Lee Ping Quan's
LONDON POUND CAKE

Serves 8 people

INGREDIENTS

6 egg whites, room temperature
12 ounces powdered sugar
12 ounces unsalted butter, room temperature
6 egg yolks, room temperature
12 ounces unbleached flour, sifted
½ tablespoon baking powder
1 tablespoon vanilla extract

We halved Chef Quan's original recipe to fit in one standard loaf pan and made several alterations. When you fold the egg whites into the batter, use a wide, shallow bowl. We tested folding the egg whites directly into the batter in the stand mixer versus taking the batter out of the stand mixer and putting it in a wide, shallow bowl. When a wide, shallow bowl was used, the result was more batter and a cake that rose higher.

To ensure that the cake rises, we suggest adding baking powder. The cake does rise without baking powder, but the technique of folding in the egg whites has to be done very gently.

Chef Quan used powdered sugar. We tested the recipe using both powdered and regular granulated sugar. The one using powdered sugar was lighter in flavor and less sweet, and the crust was smooth, whereas the one using granulated sugar had a bumpy crust. I preferred the taste of regular sugar, but we decided to stick with Chef Quan's original ingredients in this case.

This recipe does in fact take close to 2 hours to bake, as Chef Quan's did. He specified only a "slow oven," which we interpreted to be 300°F, and even at 300°F, this cake does take a long time to bake.

If you choose, you can add lemon icing after the cake is cooled. Whipped cream and fresh fruit, however, would also make a great accompaniment. Plain pound cake for breakfast is also delicious.

PREPARATION

1. Preheat oven to 300°F.
2. Prepare a greased loaf pan or a pan with parchment paper.
3. Beat egg whites until stiff. Set aside.
4. Cream together sugar and butter until slightly fluffy.
5. Add egg yolks, one at a time, until combined.
6. In a separate bowl, whisk together the flour and baking powder. Add a little at a time to the batter.
7. Add the vanilla extract. If using a stand mixer, move the batter into a wide, shallow bowl.
8. Gently fold in the egg whites to eliminate the streaks with as few strokes as possible.
9. Put the loaf pan on a sheet pan and bake in the oven. Check the cake after 60 minutes, then 80, and then 100 minutes. If the cake rises very high in volume, we suggest baking for 2 hours.

Lee Ping Quan's
LEMON ICING

INGREDIENTS

1 pound granulated sugar
1½ cups water
4 egg whites, room temperature
1 pinch salt
Juice of 1 lemon
Zest of 1 lemon

This recipe makes a lot of icing—enough for 2–3 pound cakes or 2 shortcakes, so you may want to halve the recipe. This icing can be kept refrigerated for up to 1 week.

Chef Quan's original recipe was very sparsely written, but easy to make with some additional details.

We added a pinch of salt and lemon zest for more flavor.

PREPARATION

1. Combine sugar and water and boil until a candy thermometer reads 240°F (what professional bakers call "soft-ball stage"), approximately 10–12 minutes. The sugar bubbles will gradually increase in size. The sugar mixture may turn a little light brown depending on the type of sugar you use, but do not let the sugar caramelize.
2. Meanwhile, in a stand mixer, beat the egg whites until stiff. Once stiff, turn the stand mixer down to low to keep the egg whites moving, until the sugar is ready.
3. With the stand mixer on low, slowly pour the hot mixture into the bowl, pouring along the side of the bowl to avoid splashing, until the texture is thick and creamy.
4. Add a pinch of salt.
5. Add the lemon juice and lemon zest, and combine.
6. Spread icing on cakes.

Lee Ping Quan's

JELLY ROLL
PRESIDENT COOLIDGE'S FAVORITE

Serves 6–8 people

INGREDIENTS

6 eggs
2 ounces granulated sugar
2 tablespoons cream
   (we used whipping cream)
1 teaspoon vanilla
3 ounces unbleached
   all-purpose flour
½ tablespoon baking powder
2 cups strawberry jam

This roll, like the shortcake, is slightly dense, eggy and spongy, and very sweet, so we decided to also reduce the amount of sugar by half and add baking powder as insurance to make sure it does rise a bit. The original recipe did not rely on rising agents so what is poured in the sheet pan is exactly what it looks like after baking.

We halved the recipe, as one jelly roll is generally enough for a household.

The original recipe specified beating the eggs until "stiff." We used a stand mixer with a whisk attachment and whisked on high for 5 minutes. We used sifted unbleached flour, but pastry or cake flour can also be used. Sifting the flour does matter, so do not skip this step. We switched the order as well, adding the vanilla before the flour.

PREPARATION

1. Preheat oven to 300°F. Grease or spray 1 half-sheet pan (18 x 13 inches) and then cover with parchment paper.
2. In a stand mixer with a whisk attachment, whisk eggs together for 5 minutes on high. Make sure the eggs are stiff.
3. Turn power down and add sugar, cream, and vanilla.
4. Sift flour and baking powder together, and slowly add to egg mixture until fully incorporated.
5. Pour onto the sheet pan.
6. Bake for 20 minutes (check after 15 minutes). Cool slightly.
7. Invert the sheet pan onto a towel (you may need to run a knife down the edges of the pan before you invert it). Roll the cake in a towel when warm to maintain pliability. Keep rolled until cool.
8. Unroll the cake from the towel. Spread strawberry jam on it and roll back up.
9. Sprinkle with powdered sugar or cover with lemon icing (see page 125).

Lee Ping Quan's
PEACH MUFFINS

Makes 12–24 muffins depending on fruit used

MUFFIN INGREDIENTS

3 egg whites

2–3 tablespoons butter, room temperature; use 4 tablespoons for a richer taste

½ cup sugar

3 egg yolks

1 cup sour cream

1⅓ cups flour (we used unbleached all-purpose flour)

1 teaspoon salt

½ tablespoon baking powder

4 medium peaches

CRUMB TOPPING INGREDIENTS

½ cup flour

½ cup brown sugar

½ cup unsalted butter, cold and cubed

Chef Quan had many muffin recipes, but they were not uniformly written. We could not determine whether this was intentional. We decided to start with the peach muffin recipe as that one required the fewest alterations.

Chef Quan did not use much butter in this recipe, so we increased the amount. We chose to add a crumb topping as modern tastes for muffins are much sweeter. This is optional.

Frozen fruit can be substituted.

Chef Quan uses a method for folding egg whites into the batter to create air. This requires careful technique.

See page 130 for fruit variations.

PREPARATION

1. Preheat oven to 300°F.
2. Generously butter muffin tins, or line muffin tins with liners.
3. Beat egg whites until foamy and stiff. This should take a couple of minutes. You can do this by hand, but it will take a long time. Use a beater or a stand mixer with a whisk attachment at high speed. Set aside.
4. In a stand mixer, cream butter and sugar.
5. Add egg yolks, sour cream, flour, salt, and baking powder. Move batter to a bowl with a wide, flat bottom.
6. Add 4 medium peaches, peeled and diced into small pieces. To peel, make an "X" at the bottom of each peach. Prepare a bowl of ice water. Blanch the peaches in boiling water for 30 seconds. Remove and put in ice water.
7. Fold in egg whites very gently using a large flat spatula or wide spoon, and with as few strokes as possible.
8. Place the batter in muffin tins, almost to the top.
9. If adding a crumb topping, pulse together all ingredients in a food processor. Do not overpulse. Stop when the mixture becomes a crumb-like texture, 10–15 seconds total.
10. Generously spoon on crumb topping, if using.
11. Bake for 15–20 minutes, rotating halfway. Check at 10 minutes with a toothpick. If using muffin liners, wait until the muffins are completely cool to remove them from the tins.

Lee Ping Quan's
FRUIT MUFFINS
VARIATIONS TO PEACH MUFFINS

Follow the recipe on page 129 for peach muffins, but in place of peaches other fruit can be used as follows.

Apricot
8–10 small apricots
The technique for peeling apricots is the same as for peaches.

Strawberry
1–2 pints of halved strawberries

Raspberry
1 6-ounce box of raspberries

Banana
3 mashed ripe bananas
The original recipe used cut up bananas, but we preferred mashed.

Lemon and Blueberry
Zest of 2 lemons
Juice of 1 lemon
1–2 pints blueberries

Mango and Toasted Coconut
2 pints of diced mango
½ cup toasted coconut

Lee Ping Quan's
ORANGE MARMALADE MUFFINS

Makes 12 muffins

MUFFIN INGREDIENTS

2–3 tablespoons butter
½ cup sugar
3 eggs
1 cup sour cream
1⅓ cups flour (we used unbleached all-purpose flour)
1 teaspoon salt
½ tablespoon baking powder
¾ cup orange marmalade

CRUMB TOPPING INGREDIENTS

½ cup flour
½ cup brown sugar
½ cup unsalted butter, cold and cubed

As opposed to the fruit muffin recipes, for orange marmalade muffins we decided to omit the whipping of the egg whites and to add in the entire egg. Similar to the other muffin recipes, there was not very much butter in this recipe, so we increased the amount. If you use muffin liners, wait until the muffins are completely cool to remove them from the tins.

PREPARATION

1. Preheat oven to 350°F. Generously butter muffin tins, or line muffin tins with liners.
2. In a stand mixer, cream butter and sugar.
3. Add eggs one at a time, then sour cream, flour, salt, and baking powder.
4. Stir in marmalade.
5. Place batter in muffin tins, almost to the top.
6. Pulse together crumb topping in a food processor. Do not overpulse. Stop when the mixture becomes a crumb-like texture, 10–15 seconds total.
7. Generously spoon on crumb topping.
8. Place tins on a sheet pan and put in the oven. Check at 20 minutes, rotating halfway. Add 5 minutes baking time if needed.

Lee Ping Quan's
APPLE FRITTERS
POTOMAC STYLE

Makes 8–10 fritters

INGREDIENTS

¼ cup sugar
¼ cup butter, melted
2 eggs, beaten
1 pound flour
¾ teaspoon baking powder
¼ teaspoon cinnamon
½–¾ cup milk or buttermilk
Juice of 1 lemon
1½ tablespoons vanilla extract
3 apples, peeled, and diced into small pieces
Vegetable oil for frying
Powdered sugar, cinnamon, and maple syrup for serving
Vanilla ice cream for serving

These can be eaten anytime—for breakfast or for dessert. Do not make each fritter too big; doughnut-hole-size is perfect.

PREPARATION

1. Set up a frying pan with 2 inches of oil.
2. Combine the sugar and butter and add the beaten eggs with a hand-held electric mixer or stand mixer.
3. Add the flour, baking powder, cinnamon, and milk and stir together.
4. Add the lemon juice and the vanilla extract.
5. Add the diced apples and stir until just combined.
6. Heat oil until rippling. Drop in a bit of batter to see if it bubbles.
7. Drop the fritter batter into the oil 1 tablespoon at a time and fry until brown on both sides.
8. Set aside on a sheet pan lined with paper towels. Keep in a 150°F oven until all fritters are fried.
9. Sprinkle with powdered sugar and/or cinnamon.
10. Serve with ice cream and/or maple syrup.

Lee Ping Quan's
STRAWBERRY À LA KING PIE
MRS. COOLIDGE'S FAVORITE

Makes 16 slices (2 pies)

PIE CRUSTS INGREDIENTS

1 pound flour
½–1 teaspoon salt
½ pound butter, unsalted, cold, and diced in cubes
½ cup ice water

WHIPPED CREAM INGREDIENTS

1 tablespoon mascarpone cheese or cream cheese
4 tablespoons powdered sugar
1 quart whipping cream

FILLING INGREDIENTS

2–3 quarts strawberries, halved, if the strawberries are not as ripe as you would like, macerate the fruit in ¼ cup sugar and drain any juices out before folding into whipped cream
½ cup pineapple, diced into small pieces
½ cup honeydew melon, diced into small pieces

In many of his pie recipes, Chef Quan cleverly mixed fruit chunks into the whipped cream and called the mixture "à la king." Chef Quan piped additional colored whipped cream into a flower and leaf design over the à la king mixture. This truly was a unique and easy way to make a fresh fruit pie, and whipped cream and fruit always taste good.

Use fully ripe strawberries or other fruit.

PREPARATION

1. To make the pie crusts, combine the flour and salt in a food processor.
2. Add the cubed butter, drizzle in ice water, and pulse until mixture turns into small crumbs and the dough holds together when you pinch it.
3. Place the dough in the refrigerator for 24 hours.
4. Preheat oven to 400°F.
5. Roll dough when slightly malleable and fit into two pie plates.
6. Prepare the dough to blind bake by placing either pie weights or dry beans over aluminum foil on top of the crust.
7. Bake for approximately 12 minutes.
8. Remove the aluminum foil and bake for an additional 3–5 minutes, until the crust is lightly browned. Let pie crusts cool.
9. For the whipped cream, whip cheese and powdered sugar in a stand mixer until combined.
10. Add cream until soft peaks form. Reserve two cups of whipped cream.
11. For the filling, gently fold the strawberries, pineapple, and honeydew into the whipped cream. This mixture is what we think Chef Quan called "à la king."
12. Place the à la king into the pie crusts and design to taste with the remaining 2 cups of whipped cream.
13. Refrigerate the entire pies to let them set, but you can also eat them immediately or freeze.

Lee Ping Quan's
CHOCOLATE CREAM PIE
WITH COCONUT VARIATION

Pie crust makes 16 slices (2 pies). Filling makes enough for 1 pie, double for 2.

PIE CRUSTS INGREDIENTS

1 pound flour
½–1 teaspoon salt
½ pound butter, unsalted, cold, and diced in small cubes
½ cup ice water

FILLING INGREDIENTS

1 cup sugar
¼ cup cornstarch
1 pinch salt
3 egg yolks
3 cups milk (reduced fat or whole)
2–4 ounces semisweet chocolate chips
1 tablespoon unsweetened high-quality cocoa powder
1 tablespoon unsalted butter
1 teaspoon vanilla

WHIPPED CREAM INGREDIENTS

1 tablespoon mascarpone cheese or cream cheese
4 tablespoons powdered sugar
1 quart whipping cream

OTHER INGREDIENTS

Chocolate shavings for decoration

Our first testing of Chef Quan's original recipe did not go very well. There was not enough chocolate and too much sugar for the egg yolks. The result was a block of egg mess, as the sugar could not be incorporated. We found an easier way to thicken the custard instead of tempering the eggs with a quart of boiling water.

We used the original ingredients but changed the ratio and cooking method. We omitted the addition of boiling water to temper the eggs and used milk instead. Then we heated the entire custard mixture together. We also did not fold whipped egg whites into the custard. Instead, we dropped a tablespoon of butter into the custard.

We used 2 ounces of semisweet chocolate chips, but you could increase to 4 ounces if you want more chocolate. Just be wary of the sweetness. The only new ingredient we added was cocoa powder, for a richer, deeper chocolate flavor. Use a high-quality brand.

Chef Quan did not have a recipe for stabilized whipped cream, so we used his recipe for whipped cream in the strawberry à la king pie recipe. We also used the pie crust recipe.

Continued next page

Lee Ping Quan's
CHOCOLATE CREAM PIE
WITH COCONUT VARIATION (CONTINUED)

PIE CRUST PREPARATION

1. To make the pie crusts, combine the flour and salt in a food processor.
2. Add the cubed butter, drizzle in ice water, and pulse until mixture turns into small crumbs and the dough holds together when you pinch it.
3. Place the dough in the refrigerator for 24 hours.
4. Preheat oven to 400°F.
5. Roll dough when slightly malleable and fit into two pie plates.
6. Prepare the dough to blind bake by placing either pie weights or dry beans over aluminum foil on top of the crust.
7. Bake for approximately 12 minutes.
8. Remove the aluminum foil and bake for an additional 3–5 minutes until the crust is lightly browned. Let pie crusts cool.

FILLING PREPARATION

1. In a medium saucepan, combine sugar, cornstarch, and salt.
2. Add the egg yolks, and whisk in the milk.
3. Add chocolate chips and cocoa powder.
4. Heat custard mixture over medium heat. Whisk frequently.
5. Change to a rubber spatula to make sure no mixture gets stuck to the sides of the pan.
6. Take off heat when the mixture is thick to your desired consistency.
7. Immediately put the mixture in a bowl and fold in the butter and vanilla.
8. Cool until almost room temperature.
9. Cover bowl with plastic wrap and refrigerate until completely cool.
10. Ladle chocolate mixture into baked and cooled pie crust.

WHIPPED CREAM PREPARATION

1. Whip cheese and powdered sugar in a stand mixer until combined.
2. Add cream until soft peaks form.
3. Serve with dollops of whipped cream on top or on the side. If the whipped cream is added as a second layer, then refrigerate the pie for a couple of hours before serving.
4. For decoration, you can add chocolate shavings or sprinkled cocoa powder.
5. Pies can be frozen once cooled.

COCONUT VARIATION

FILLING INGREDIENTS (FOR 1 PIE)

1 cup milk (reduced fat or whole)
2 cups coconut milk
4 ounces coconut, toasted
1 cup sugar
¼ cup cornstarch
1 pinch salt
3 egg yolks
1 tablespoon unsalted butter
1 teaspoon vanilla

FILLING PREPARATION

1. Heat milks gently and add toasted coconut.
2. Turn off heat and seep for 30 minutes.
3. Strain out coconut.
4. In a medium saucepan, combine sugar, cornstarch, and salt.
5. Add the egg yolks and whisk in the milk mixture.
6. Heat custard mixture over medium heat. Whisk frequently.
7. Change to a rubber spatula to make sure no mixture gets stuck to the sides of the pan.
8. Take off heat when the mixture is thickened to your desired consistency.
9. Immediately put the mixture in a bowl and fold in the butter and vanilla.
10. Cool until almost room temperature.
11. Cover bowl with plastic wrap and refrigerate until completely cool.
12. Ladle coconut mixture into baked and cooled pie crust.

Lee Ping Quan's
LEMON SQUALL

Serves 8 people

INGREDIENTS

6 lemons (seedless lemons make your life a lot easier)
6 limes
3 quarts water
1½ pounds sugar

This is a great nonalcoholic drink for a party or a homemade summer drink to keep in the refrigerator for the family.

We found the word "squall" interesting, and a quick internet search turns up an association with citrus craft beers.

We were tempted to skip boiling the lime rinds in the water, but gently boiling them did make a difference in flavor. And include the lemon rinds too if you want (but we would not recommend too many as that might make the drink too bitter). The rinds supercharge the flavor of the water, making it super sour.

There is a slight bitterness, but that is the signature of a natural drink, and it is offset by the sweetness of the sugar. We used less sugar to make it less sweet, and it was delicious. Children would be happy with the full amount. The original recipe required putting "ice cubes in while whipping to make cold." Thank goodness, with modern refrigeration, there is no need.

PREPARATION

1. Shave the rinds from the lemons and limes.
2. Drop them into boiling water for 2½ minutes.
3. Strain the rinds out of the water.
4. Squeeze juice from lemons and limes.
5. Add the lemon juice and lime juice to the water.
6. Add the sugar and mix all together.
7. Refrigerate.
8. Pour over ice.

More from

Navy, Staff, and Guest Chefs

Edward Lee's

MARYLAND CRAB CAKES
ON MATCHSTICK VEGETABLES WITH FENNEL TOMATO
STATE DINNER FOR SOUTH KOREA

Serves 6 people

CRAB CAKE INGREDIENTS

1 egg
¼ cup mayonnaise
1 tablespoon fresh parsley, chopped
2 teaspoons Dijon mustard
1 teaspoon Old Bay seasoning
1½ teaspoons fresh lemon juice
Zest of 1 lemon
⅛ teaspoon salt
1 pinch black pepper
1 pound fresh lump crab meat
½ cup panko bread crumbs
2 tablespoons olive oil for frying

VINAIGRETTE INGREDIENTS

1 cup olive oil
⅓ cup rice vinegar
1 tablespoon lemon juice
2 teaspoons *gochujang*
1 pinch sugar
Salt and pepper
¼ cup chives, finely chopped

FENNEL TOMATO INGREDIENTS

1 cup fennel, finely chopped
2 Roma tomatoes, finely chopped, seeds removed
½ cup dill, finely chopped
¼ cup fennel fronds, finely chopped
1 tablespoon lemon juice
Zest of 1 orange
¼ teaspoon ground cumin
1 tablespoon olive oil
Salt and pepper

VEGETABLE INGREDIENTS

½ pound cabbage cut into matchsticks
½ pound yellow bell peppers cut into matchsticks
½ pound kohlrabi cut into matchsticks
½ pound seedless cucumbers (skin on) cut into matchsticks

CRAB CAKE PREPARATION

1. In a bowl, whisk together the egg, mayonnaise, parsley, mustard, Old Bay, lemon juice, lemon zest, salt, and pepper.
2. Add crab meat and panko crumbs and gently mix together.
3. Let chill, covered, in the refrigerator for 4 hours.
4. Remove from refrigerator and form into loose crab cakes.
5. Heat a cast-iron pan with the olive oil over medium-high heat.
6. Add crab cakes to pan and cook for about 5 minutes on one side, flip, and cook for another 4 minutes until both sides are golden brown.
7. Drain on paper towels and reserve warm in a 150°F oven.

VINAIGRETTE PREPARATION

1. Mix olive oil, vinegar, lemon juice, *gochujang*, sugar, salt, and pepper thoroughly.
2. Just before serving mix in the chopped chives.

FENNEL TOMATO PREPARATION

1. Combine all ingredients and chill in refrigerator for at least 3 hours.

TO PLATE

1. Arrange the matchstick vegetables next to each other.
2. Place fried crab cake on top.
3. Dress the vegetables and crab cake with the *gochujang* vinaigrette.
4. Place rounded tablespoon of fennel tomato on top of crab cake.

Edward Lee's

CHILLED YELLOW SQUASH SOUP
WITH CURED STRAWBERRIES AND PERILLA OIL
STATE DINNER FOR SOUTH KOREA

Serves 6 people

CURED STRAWBERRY INGREDIENTS

1 pound fresh strawberries, washed and trimmed
½ teaspoon kosher salt
½ teaspoon sugar

SOUP INGREDIENTS

2 tablespoons olive oil
½ cup onions, chopped
2 pounds yellow squash, roughly chopped
4 sprigs of thyme, stem removed, finely chopped
2 cups vegetable stock
½ cup sour cream
2 teaspoons salt
Maldon salt
Fresh cracked pepper

PERILLA OIL GARNISH

Shredded fresh perilla leaf
2 tablespoons to ¼ cup olive oil

CURED STRAWBERRY PREPARATION

1. Slice the strawberries and place them in a glass bowl.
2. Sprinkle the salt and sugar over the strawberries.
3. Gently toss the strawberries with your fingers, making sure not to crush them.
4. Leave them to cure for 40 minutes at room temperature. If left for any longer, they will start to get too soft.

SOUP PREPARATION

1. In a large skillet, heat the olive oil over medium heat.
2. Add the onions and cook until translucent, about 2 minutes.
3. Add the yellow squash and the thyme. Sauté for another 3 minutes.
4. Add the vegetable stock and bring to a boil.
5. Simmer for 10 minutes or until the squash is completely soft all the way through.
6. Take the mixture off the heat and let it cool for a few minutes.
7. Transfer the mixture to a blender.
8. Add the sour cream and salt.
9. Purée on high for about 2 minutes.
10. Check the consistency. If the mixture is a little gritty, strain it through a fine mesh sieve.
11. Chill the soup in the refrigerator for 2 hours or overnight.
12. To make perilla oil, blanch perilla leaves and purée with olive oil until a pureé like consistency is achieved. Let steep for 1 hour. Strain out the leaves and discard.
13. To serve, ladle chilled soup into small cups. Top with one cured strawberry slice. Add Maldon salt and fresh black pepper over the top. Add perilla leaf garnish. Drizzle a little perilla oil on top.

Edward Lee's

BRAISED BEEF SHORT RIBS
STATE DINNER FOR SOUTH KOREA

Serves 6 people

INGREDIENTS

8 pounds English-cut short ribs
4 tablespoons corn oil
2 tablespoons sesame oil
2 large onions, chopped
8 cloves garlic, chopped
1 large knob of ginger, peeled and minced, about 1 tablespoon
6 carrots, peeled and roughly chopped
6 celery sticks, roughly chopped
1 cup cooking wine
2 cups soy sauce
6 cups chicken stock
4 tablespoons sugar
4 teaspoons honey
2 teaspoons black pepper
¾ cup pine nuts
2 tablespoons butter for sauce

PREPARATION

1. In a large roasting pan (you may need to use two burners), sear the short ribs in the oil mixture until browned on both sides.
2. Add the onions, garlic, ginger, carrots, and celery.
3. Add cooking wine.
4. Cook for 3 minutes.
5. Add the soy sauce and chicken stock.
6. Bring to a slow simmer and stir in the sugar, honey, and black pepper.
7. Simmer, partially covered and turning ribs occasionally, for about 2 hours, until meat is falling off bone and sauce is reduced.
8. Turn off heat and let meat cool in the liquid, about 2 hours.
9. Remove short ribs.
10. Transfer the meat out of the pan and set aside. Portion into 5 ounce portions.
11. Meanwhile, strain liquid and discard solids. Skim fat off the liquid.
12. Cook the pine nuts in about 1 cup of sauce for about 15 minutes. Reserve to the side until ready to plate.
13. Put the remaining sauce in a small pot, cook to reduce for 20 minutes, and add butter. Keep warm until ready for service.
14. To serve each portion, spoon sauce and sprinkle pine nuts over short ribs.
15. Serve with butter bean grits (see page 146) and sorghum-glazed carrots (see page 148).

Edward Lee's
BUTTER BEAN GRITS
STATE DINNER FOR SOUTH KOREA

Serves 6 people

INGREDIENTS

2 tablespoons olive oil
1 shallot, finely diced
4 cloves garlic, chopped
2 cups butter beans, shelled
1 cup water
½ cup tahini
¼ cup lemon juice
1 tablespoon soy sauce
1½ teaspoons salt
1 teaspoon ground cumin

PREPARATION

1. In a large saucepan, heat the olive oil over medium heat.
2. Add the shallot and garlic and sauté for 2 minutes until soft.
3. Add the beans and cook for 2 minutes.
4. Add the water, tahini, lemon juice, soy sauce, salt, and cumin.
5. Stir and simmer for 6 to 8 minutes.
6. Transfer the contents to a food processor and purée until you get a thick crumbly purée that resembles grits.
7. Keep warm in a pot on the stove until ready to serve.

Edward Lee's

SORGHUM-GLAZED CARROTS
STATE DINNER FOR SOUTH KOREA

Serves 6 people

INGREDIENTS

4 tablespoons butter
1 pound carrots, baby tricolor, tops trimmed
4 tablespoons brown sugar
3 tablespoons minced fresh ginger
1½ ounces bourbon
Juice of 1 orange
2 teaspoons salt
Pepper to taste

PREPARATION

1. In a large skillet, heat the butter over high heat.
2. Add the carrots and sauté for about 6 minutes.
3. Add the brown sugar and the minced ginger and cook until the brown sugar melts, about 2 minutes.
4. Add bourbon and the orange juice slowly and scrape bits off bottom of the pan to deglaze.
5. Cook until carrots are fork tender and the liquid has been reduced to syrup, about 6–8 minutes.
6. Season with salt and pepper.
7. Serve as an accompaniment to braised beef short ribs (see page 145) or slow cooked brisket.

Anita Lo's

BUTTER-POACHED MAINE LOBSTER
WITH FRESH RICE NOODLE ROLLS
STATE DINNER FOR CHINA

Serves 12 people

INGREDIENTS

12 1-pound Maine (sub-Canadian, cold water) lobsters, tomalley (the green stuff in the heads of the lobsters) removed and reserved, tails and claws cooked and shelled, heads and shells reserved, roe reserved, microwaved, and passed through a fine mesh strainer to make a powder

2 pounds diced cold butter mounted/emulsified into simmering lobster stock to make a beurre monté

6 fresh *hor fun* noodle sheets (do not refrigerate)

Spinach mixture:
- 1½ pounds spinach, blanched, shocked, and squeezed dry
- 4 large leek whites, cleaned and cut into 1 centimeter squares, sweated in butter, and seasoned with salt
- 24 large shiitake caps (sliced and sautéed in oil and butter, seasoned with salt and pepper)
- Lobster knuckles and meat scraps from above

Oyster sauce to taste

SAUCE INGREDIENTS

2 cups white wine
1 large shallot, finely diced
1 large clove garlic, smashed
1 sprig tarragon
4 ripe plum tomatoes, peeled (substitute a good quality canned)
Reserved lobster heads and shells
2½ quarts lobster stock
1 pound butter, cubed
Black pepper to taste
1 pinch cayenne
Lemon juice to taste
Salt or sugar to taste
Equal parts tomalley to heavy cream, brought to a boil and strained
Small tarragon leaves for garnish

PREPARATION

1. Make the rice noodle rolls within a few hours of serving. Best not to refrigerate the rolls as the noodle will harden and will easily break.
2. Mix the blanched, shocked spinach, sweated leeks, and sautéed shiitakes with the excess lobster meat.
3. Season to taste with oyster sauce and freshly ground black pepper.
4. Cut rice noodle sheets into four pieces (some will be unusable).
5. Cover with a thin layer of the spinach mixture, leaving a 2-centimeter margin on the top and bottom.
6. Roll up tightly to form cylinders about 4 centimeters in diameter.
7. Cut into 5 centimeter high rounds. The inside should be a spiral. Use two per serving.
8. For the sauce, in a large pot, place the white wine, shallot, garlic, and tarragon and reduce by three-fourths.
9. Add the tomatoes, lobster heads and shells, and lobster stock. Reduce by two-thirds.
10. Strain, pushing any pulp through and continue to reduce until about ¾ cup remains.
11. Whisk in a little at a time to emulsify with the butter while the base is simmering, then season to taste with pepper, cayenne, lemon juice, and salt or sugar, if necessary. Keep warm.
12. Reheat rice noodle rolls in a steamer. Reheat half the tail and a claw in the beurre monté, seasoned with salt, pepper, and lemon.
13. To serve, place around ⅔ ounces in the center of a rectangular plate and form a smaller rectangle with it.
14. Top with the reheated rice noodle rolls and the lobster to one side, then make a dot on each side with the tomalley sauce, sprinkled with a bit of roe.
15. Garnish with 2–3 tarragon leaves and serve.

Anita Lo's

MUSHROOM SOUP
WITH ACORN SQUASH AND ACORN JELLY
STATE DINNER FOR CHINA

Serves 6–8 people

INGREDIENTS

1 quart chicken stock
½ cup dried black trumpet mushrooms (Regalis brand)
¼ cup dried porcini
1 quart mixed wild mushrooms, cleaned and sliced
¼ cup Shaoxing wine, or to taste
1 can black winter truffle *tuber melanosporum* juice (optional)
Mushroom soy to taste (Happy Boy brand)
Salt and pepper to taste
Fresh lemon juice to taste (just a tad to balance)

1 large acorn squash, peeled, seeded, and cut into small triangles, or any uniform shape
2–4 tablespoons olive or vegetable oil
Salt and pepper

Acorn squash seeds from the squash, rinsed
1–2 tablespoons olive or vegetable oil
Salt and pepper

GARNISH

Pumpkin seed oil
Roasted acorn squash seeds
Diagonal cut thinly sliced scallions, white part (use a bit of the pale green part, too)
8 ounces Korean acorn jelly, cut into cubes (optional)

PREPARATION

1. In a Dutch oven bring the stock, dried mushrooms, wild mushrooms, and Shaoxing wine to a boil.
2. Simmer until well flavored and the mushrooms are cooked through.
3. Add the truffle juice and season to taste with the mushroom soy, salt, pepper, and a touch of lemon.
4. Roast the acorn squash on a baking sheet with oil, salt, and pepper in one layer at 400°F for approximately 30 to 45 minutes until cooked through.
5. Reduce heat to 300°F and roast the acorn squash seeds. Check at 15 minutes until crisp.
6. To serve, reheat the acorn squash and the soup and put acorn squash into the soup.
7. Garnish with the pumpkin seed oil, seeds, scallions, and acorn jelly.

Anita Lo's

GRILLED LOIN OF LAMB
WITH ROASTED GARLIC FRIED MILK
STATE DINNER FOR CHINA

Serves 12 people

MARINADE INGREDIENTS

1 spanish onion, sliced
2 tablespoons garlic, freshly chopped
1 cup lime juice
¼ cup Korean ground chili (*gochu garu*—coarse)
¼ cup nonflavored oil

SAUCE INGREDIENTS

3 shallots, sliced
3 large garlic cloves, smashed
½ bottle red wine
1½ gallons veal stock
Salt and pepper

MILK INGREDIENTS

24 ounces evaporated milk
6 cups whole milk
⅔ cup roasted garlic purée (very little color)
6 ounces cornstarch
3 tablespoons gelatin, bloomed with 5 tablespoons water
2 tablespoons thyme leaves
2 tablespoons scallion green, finely chopped
Salt and pepper to taste

LAMB INGREDIENTS

12 6-ounce lamb loins, cleaned
Salt and pepper

BATTER

3 cups flour
½ cup cornstarch
1 tablespoon baking powder
Salt and pepper
3 cups very cold soda water

CHILI OIL

½ cup nonflavored oil such as canola
3 tablespoons Korean ground chili (*gochu garu*, coarse)
Salt and pepper

BROCCOLI

8 cloves garlic, chopped and heated in oil
2 pounds Chinese broccoli (*gai lan*), cleaned and sliced
Water or chicken stock as needed

PREPARATION

1. Mix the marinade ingredients together and toss with the lamb loins to coat. Allow to marinate at least 3 hours or up to overnight.
2. To make the sauce, place the browned lamb shank (this can be done in an oven or in a pot) along with the shallots, garlic, and wine. Reduce by three-fourths.
3. Add the veal stock and bring to a boil.
4. Skim and turn to a simmer, cook, skimming occasionally until well flavored and thickened.
5. Strain and season to taste with salt and pepper.
6. To make the milk, mix together milks, garlic purée, and cornstarch in a pot and bring to a boil, whisking constantly.
7. When thickened and cornstarch flavor is cooked out, remove from heat and add gelatin, thyme, scallions, salt, and pepper. Stir until uniform and gelatin is melted.
8. Pour into a greased hotel pan, cover, and refrigerate until set and cold.
9. Cut into 3-inch squares.
10. To make the batter, in a medium-size bowl, mix the dry ingredients. Add wet ingredients.
11. To make the chili oil, slowly heat the chili and oil together until just bubbling. Turn off the heat. When cool, season to taste with salt and pepper.
12. Preheat grill to high.
13. Scrape off the excess onions and marinade from the lamb, leaving the chili behind.
14. Season on all sides with salt and pepper and grill to desired temperature.
15. Set on a rack to rest at least 5 minutes or up to 10 minutes.
16. Batter the squares of "milk" and deep fry until golden and crunchy. Sauté the broccoli in oil and garlic, season with salt, adding a little water or chicken stock as needed.

Anita Lo's

POPPY SEED BREAD AND BUTTER PUDDING
WITH MEYER LEMON CURD
STATE DINNER FOR CHINA

Serves 8 people

PUDDING INGREDIENTS

3 quarts cubed (about ¾ inch per side) old plain French bread, bottom and top crusts removed

½ cup butter (1 stick), melted

2 tablespoons sugar

5 large eggs, beaten with a pinch of salt

1¾ cups sugar

3 tablespoons rum

½ vanilla bean, scraped seeds

1 quart heavy cream

1½ tablespoons poppy seeds

CURD INGREDIENTS

4 large eggs beaten with a pinch of salt

1½ cups sugar

1 cup Meyer lemon juice with zest

¾ cup (1½ sticks) butter, cut into pieces

More Meyer lemon juice and zest to thin to sauce consistency

PUDDING PREPARATION

1. In a large mixing bowl, toss the cubed bread with the melted butter and the 2 tablespoons of sugar.
2. In a separate mixing bowl, mix the eggs with the 1¾ cups sugar, beating until lightened.
3. Mix the rum with the vanilla bean seeds in a small bowl and stir to break up the seeds and add to egg mixture.
4. Add the heavy cream and poppy seeds to the egg mixture and stir.
5. Pour over the bread and stir so that the bread is coated on all sides.
6. Cover and allow to sit overnight for the bread to soak up the custard.
7. The next day, bake at 325°F for 30 minutes (check at 20 minutes) until browned, crispy, and set.
8. Allow to cool completely before covering and refrigerating.
9. When fully chilled, cut into diamond-shaped pieces.
10. To serve, reheat in a 350°F oven until hot in the center and serve with the Meyer lemon curd.

CURD PREPARATION

1. In a stainless steel bowl, beat the eggs with the sugar.
2. Add the Meyer lemon juice and zest.
3. Place over boiling water and heat, stirring constantly.
4. Add the butter little by little until it melts and the mixture is thickened, stirring constantly.
5. Transfer to a cool container and chill.
6. Add more Meyer lemon juice to thin to sauce consistency once the mixture is chilled.

Ariel De Guzman's

CHAPARRAL WILTED SPINACH SALAD

Serves 4 people

INGREDIENTS

3 cups spinach, washed, picked over, stems removed, spin-dried
½ cup bacon, diced
3 tablespoons olive oil
½ cup onion, diced
½ cup mushrooms, sliced
¼ cup cognac
1 tablespoon Dijon-style mustard
Juice of ½ lemon
2 tablespoons sour cream

Chef Ariel De Guzman said this salad was a favorite of President George H. W. Bush.

PREPARATION

1. Put spinach in a large bowl. Set aside.
2. In a skillet over medium heat, cook bacon until brown and crispy. Remove crispy bacon bits with slotted spoon; set aside. Discard bacon grease.
3. In the same skillet over medium heat, heat the olive oil.
4. Add onion and mushrooms and cook until mushrooms are tender.
5. Remove from heat and pour in cognac.
6. Return to heat and tip pan to ignite cognac. When flames die down, add mustard, lemon juice, and sour cream; stir well.
7. Pour hot dressing over spinach.
8. Cover bowl with aluminum foil for 4 minutes until spinach wilts.
9. Toss lightly and serve immediately.

Ariel De Guzman's

PUFFED CHEESE ROLLS

Makes 7 dozen cheese rolls

INGREDIENTS

2¼ cups milk
2 cups plus 2 tablespoons grated Parmesan cheese, or 2 (6-ounce) packages
2½ cups corn oil
5 large eggs
1¼ tablespoons salt
2⅓ cups yucca sweet flour
1¾ cups yucca bitter flour

Chef Ariel De Guzman explained that the finished breads look like puffed pastries or éclairs. They tend to collapse when removed from heat prematurely. Turn oven off and leave in oven to produce crispier and firmer puffed rolls. The centers will remain hollow, soft, and cheesy.

Unused batter keeps for weeks if well covered under refrigeration. To reuse batter, whisk until thick again before filling muffin tins. Sweet and bitter yucca flour can be purchased from any Brazilian store and many specialty markets.

Do not be alarmed by the amount of salt and oil needed in the recipe. It gets absorbed and blends well with the yucca flour.

PREPARATION

1. Heat oven to 375°F.
2. Spray mini-muffin tins with pan spray.
3. In saucepan, heat milk to a simmer. Do not boil.
4. In a food processor, grind Parmesan to extra-fine granules.
5. Add corn oil and process until smooth.
6. With processor on, add eggs, one at a time, and process until mixture becomes very thick.
7. Transfer cheese-egg mixture to the bowl of a stand mixer fitted with the whisk.
8. Beat at slow speed while adding heated milk in a steady stream.
9. Add salt.
10. Continue beating on medium speed for 3 minutes.
11. In a large bowl, carefully combine sweet and bitter yucca flours and gradually add to liquid mixture. Mixture will be lumpy at this point. Beat at high speed for 5 minutes, or until batter has the consistency of a thick pancake batter.
12. Fill muffin cups to the rim.
13. Bake for 20 minutes.
14. Serve piping hot.

Ariel De Guzman's
WHITE HOUSE CHEESE BLISTERS

Makes 6–8 dozen blisters

INGREDIENTS

1 cup all-purpose flour
½ teaspoon salt
¼ teaspoon cayenne pepper
8 tablespoons (1 stick) unsalted butter, at room temperature
1 cup grated cheddar cheese
3 tablespoons ice water

Chef Ariel De Guzman said this recipe was shared by the White House Mess stewards with the stewards at the vice president's house. These cracker-like "blisters" are cut into assorted shapes before baking. You may make these blisters by rolling the dough ½ inch thick and cutting into 4-inch sticks. Twist sticks as you transfer them to baking sheets if you like.

PREPARATION

1. Heat oven to 425°F.
2. In a bowl, sift together flour, salt, and cayenne pepper.
3. Cut in butter and cheese until mixture resembles coarse cornmeal.
4. Add water 1 tablespoon at a time, mixing well with a fork after each addition, until mixture forms a soft dough.
5. Form dough into a ball, wrap with plastic, and chill for 30 minutes, until firm and easy to handle.
6. On a floured work surface, roll dough.
7. Cut into strips.
8. Brush off excess flour.
9. Transfer strips to baking sheets and bake for about 10 minutes, until golden brown.
10. Biscuits will puff and blister during baking.

Ariel De Guzman's
PORK ADOBO

Serves 4 people

INGREDIENTS

2½–3 pounds pork butt
½ cup rice vinegar or cider vinegar
¼ cup soy sauce
10–15 black peppercorns, cracked
6 garlic gloves, crushed
2 bay leaves
2 teaspoons cornstarch
1 teaspoon sugar
1 tablespoon water

Chef Ariel De Guzman explained that Adobo is a very popular dish from the Republic of the Philippines. The dish is aromatic and mouthwatering during and after the cooking process. A Philippine buffet will always offer this dish as one of the many entrées. To Filipinos, the absence of this dish on a buffet is a sin.

PREPARATION

1. Cut pork butt into large chunks; trim excess fat and discard. Rinse pork chunks in running cold water and transfer pieces directly to a large heavy-bottomed saucepan.
2. Add vinegar, soy sauce, cracked black peppercorns, and garlic.
3. Toss to coat all meat pieces.
4. Add bay leaves.
5. Simmer for 25 minutes or until seasoning sauce is reduced by half and bubbly.
6. Remove saucepan from heat.
7. Discard bay leaves.
8. In a small bowl, combine cornstarch, sugar, and water to make a paste.
9. Stir into pork.
10. Return to saucepan to heat and simmer for 10 minutes.
11. Serve with steamed rice.

VARIATION

Follow pork adobo recipe, substituting pork spareribs (cut across bones to make smaller pieces) for the pork butt. Simmer for at least 45 minutes to ensure meat is done and liquid is reduced to a thick sauce. Skim off and discard grease and bay leaves.

Cristeta Comerford's

CAULIFLOWER MAC AND CHEESE

Serves 3–4 people

INGREDIENTS

½ pound whole wheat penne pasta
¼ head cauliflower, cut into florets
8 ounces sharp Cheddar cheese, shredded
1 ounce Parmesan cheese, grated
½ cup 1% or 2% milk
Salt and freshly ground black pepper
1½ teaspoons fresh flat-leaf parsley, chopped

This Chef Comerford recipe appeared in First Lady Michelle Obama's book, American Grown. *Chef Cristeta Comerford wrote "Using pureéd cauliflower gives this variation on the classic mac and cheese a deliciously creamy texture without the extra fat and calories, and the whole wheat pasta has a nutty flavor. The pasta and cauliflower can be cooked at the same time, and since you're not baking the dish, it's an easy weeknight treat. Serve it as a side; or just add a salad and you've got dinner. If you're feeding a family with big appetites, the recipe is easily doubled."*

PREPARATION

1. Bring a large pot of salted water to a boil and cook the pasta according to the package directions until al dente. Drain and set aside.
2. Bring a medium pot of salted water to a boil, add the cauliflower, and cook for 5 to 7 minutes, or until soft. Drain. Place the cauliflower in a blender and purée.
3. In a medium pan over medium heat, place the pasta, the cauliflower purée, the cheeses, and the milk. Stir gently to combine and continue stirring until the cheese is melted.
4. Season with salt and pepper. Sprinkle the chopped parsley over the mac and cheese and serve immediately.

Irineo Esperancilla's
PANCIT

Serves 4–6 people

INGREDIENTS

1 package *pancit canton* or *sotanghon* (noodles)
1 tablespoon vegetable oil
1 garlic clove, sliced
1 onion, sliced into thin bite-size strips
2 carrots, sliced into thin bite-size strips
2 cups green beans, fresh or frozen, petite or whole
2 cups cabbage, shredded
2 cups chicken, cooked and shredded (dark meat/thighs preferred)
1½ cups chicken broth
1 teaspoon salt
1 teaspoon pepper
1 teaspoon *achuete annato* powder
Soy sauce to taste
1 lemon for garnish, cut into slices
Oil for sautéing

Pancit—a dish made up of rice flour noodles, meat, chopped vegetables, and soy sauce—is an extremely popular noodle dish in the Philippines. In Hokkien, a regional language in several Southeast Asian countries, pancit means "something conveniently cooked." If mung bean noodles are used, this same dish is called sotanghon. In his memoir, Irineo Esperancilla shared this anecdote about First Lady Lou Henry Hoover and the Filipino national dish: "On another occasion, Mrs. Hoover came into the kitchen while the Filipino cooks were making a native dish, sotanghon. Mrs. Hoover delighted in tasting the Filipino noodles; she even asked for more and ate a full serving."— Melinda Dart, *A Glimpse of Greatness*

PREPARATION

1. Soak pancit noodles in warm water for 8-10 minutes; drain and set aside.
2. In a large pan, add vegetable oil, and sauté garlic and onions over medium heat; add carrots and green beans. Continue to sauté until vegetables are tender.
3. Add cabbage and chicken to pan. Continue to sauté until cabbage is tender. Stir in 1 cup chicken broth.
4. Lower heat and fold in noodles. Add remaining chicken broth.
5. Add salt, pepper, and *achuete*. Stir fry all ingredients well.
6. Remove from heat.
7. Add soy sauce to taste. Garnish with lemon slices.

Masako Morishita's

GARLIC EDAMAME DUMPLINGS

Makes approximately 70 dumplings

INGREDIENTS

1 pound edamame, shelled
2–3 garlic cloves
1 tablespoons salt
⅓ cup extra-virgin olive oil
2 tablespoons soy sauce
2 tablespoons lemon juice
6 tablespoons mayonnaise
Dumpling wrappers
Small dish of water

GARNISH

Extra-virgin olive oil
Lemon
Parmesan cheese
Black pepper
Chives, finely chopped

Masako Morishita, a Japanese heritage executive chef based in Washington, D.C., prepared this dish for a luncheon hosted by Vice President Kamala Harris and Secretary of State Anthony Blinken for Japanese Prime Minister Kishida Fumio in 2024.

PREPARATION

1. Combine edamame, garlic, and salt in a blender or food processor until well mixed.
2. Add olive oil, soy sauce, and lemon juice. When everything has combined, add mayonnaise and blend again. Scrape the mixture into a bowl.
3. Hold a dumping wrapper on your palm and place about 1 teaspoon of the filling in the center of the wrapper. Dip a finger in the water and moisten the edge of the dumpling skin. Fold in half, then fold the edge of the dumplings like small waves using your fingers to seal.
4. Place a large pot of water on the stove, add salt, a drizzle of olive oil, and bring to a boil. Boil dumplings until they float, approximately 1½ minutes (timing may vary depending on the different types of dumpling wrappers).
5. Remove cooked dumplings from the pot, strain, and place them on a plate. Garnish with a drizzle of olive oil, a squeeze of lemon juice, grated Parmesan cheese, and cracked black pepper. Top with chives and enjoy!

Notes

CHAPTER ONE

The epigraph is quoted in Jackie Martin, "Ah Loy, Chef on *Mayflower* for 24 Years, Tells How He Pleased Four Presidents," *Washington Daily News*, April 1, 1929, 3.

1. Charles B. Doleac, foreword to *An Uncommon Commitment to Peace: Portsmouth Peace Treaty of 1905* (Portsmouth, N.H.: Japan-America Society of New Hampshire, 2006), 2.
2. "Treaty of Portsmouth," *Britannica*, www.britannica.com.
3. Tyler Dennett, *Roosevelt and the Russo-Japanese War: A Critical Study of American Policy in Eastern Asia in 1902–5, Based Primarily upon the Private Papers of Theodore Roosevelt* (1925; reprint, Gloucester, Mass.: Peter Smith, 1959), 239.
4. Kenneth T. Walsh, "Time on the Water: The Floating White House and the Presidents at Sea," *White House History Quarterly*, no. 71 (Fall 2023): 11.
5. Walter W. Jaffee, *The Presidential Yacht Potomac* (Palo Alto, Calif.: Glencannon Press, 1998), 15.
6. Lee Ping Quan, *To a President's Taste: Being the Reminiscences and Recipes of Lee Ping Quan, Ex-President's Steward on the Presidential Yacht, U.S.S. Mayflower, as Told to Jim Miller* (Emmaus, Pa.: Rodale Press, 1939), 6.
7. *Filipinos in the United States Navy*, report prepared by the Bureau of Naval Personnel, October 1976, online at Naval History and Command website, www.history.navy.mil.
8. *Uncommon Commitment to Peace*, 40.
9. Muster Roll of the Crew of the USS *Dolphin* on the 30th Day of September 1905, Muster Rolls of Naval Ships and Shore Establishments, January 1898–June 30, 1939, Records of the Bureau of Naval Personnel, Record Group 24, NAID: 563603, National Archives, Washington, D.C. These names, and the names from the USS Mayflower muster rolls, given below, are spelled as best as can be deciphered from ship logs, which are difficult to read.
10. "Peace Envoys Depart," *Chambersburg (Pa.) Public Opinion*, August 7, 1905, 4.
11. Quoted in Arthur F. Degreve, "U.S. *Mayflower* Leaves for Navy Yard to Be Decommissioned," *Butte Montana Standard*, April 4, 1929, 2.
12. Muster Roll of the Crew of the USS *Mayflower* on the 30th Day of September 1905, Muster Rolls of Naval Ships and Shore Establishments, January 1898–June 30, 1939, Records of the Bureau of Naval Personnel, Record Group 24, NAID: 572847, National Archives.
13. Cheuk Kwan, *Have You Eaten Yet: Stories from Chinese Restaurants Around the World* (New York: Pegasus, 2023), 1.
14. Muster Roll of the Crew of the USS *Mayflower* on the 23rd Day of June 1900, Muster Rolls of Naval Ships and Shore Establishments, January 1898–June 30, 1939, Records of the Bureau of Naval Personnel, Record Group 24, NAID: 572847, National Archives; "Denies Slave Story," *New York Tribune*, July 25, 1909, 14; "Masa Watanabe Dies; Taft's Chef on Yacht," *Washington Evening Star*, January 6, 1947, A10.
15. Reproduced in *Uncommon Commitment to Peace*, 40.
16. Frederick S. Harrod, "Jim Crow in the Navy 1798–1941," *Naval Institute Proceedings* 105, no. 9 (September 1979), online at U.S. Naval Institute website, www.usni.org.
17. *U.S. Navy Cook-Book*, 2nd ed. (Annapolis: U.S. Naval Institute, January 1920).
18. "Dinner to Roosevelts Aboard the *Mayflower*," *Washington Times Herald*, February 6, 1906, 1.
19. *The Cook Book of the United States Navy* (Washington, D.C.: U.S. Government Printing Office, 1927), 23, 32.
20. Martin, "Ah Loy, Chef on *Mayflower* for 24 Years."
21. Degreve, "U.S. *Mayflower* Leaves for Navy Yard to Be Decommissioned."
22. Martin, "Ah Loy, Chef on *Mayflower* for 24 Years."
23. Quoted in Degreve, "U.S. *Mayflower* Leaves for Navy Yard to Be Decommissioned."
24. "Out of a Job," *Napa (Calif.) Journal*, June 15, 1929, 1.
25. Martin, "Ah Loy, Chef on *Mayflower* for 24 Years."
26. "Steward to Four Presidents Dies," *Washington Evening Star*, December 30, 1934, 16.
27. "Japanese Gets Stewardship in Congress Club," *Washington Times Herald*, June 15, 1922, 3.
28. "Rockville and Vicinity," *Washington Evening Star*, June 28, 1907, 11.
29. Ibid.; "An International Affair," *Baltimore Sun*, June 29, 1907, 11; "Jap Steward on *Mayflower* Has His Marital Troubles," *Washington Herald*, August 20, 1918, 3.
30. "Jap Steward on *Mayflower* Has His Marital Troubles."
31. "Marriage Licenses," *Baltimore Sun*, August 18, 1921, 12.
32. "Japanese Gets Stewardship in Congress Club."
33. *Personal Justice Denied: Report of the Commission on Wartime Relocation and Internment of Civilians* (Washington, D.C.: Civil Liberties Public Education Fund; Seattle: University of Washington Press, 1997), 30.
34. Masakazu Iwata, "The Japanese Immigrants in California Agriculture," *Agricultural History* 36, no. 1 (January 1996): 25–37.
35. "Name Is Backward," *Washington Evening Star*, January 20, 1921, 4.
36. *Takao Ozawa v. United States*, 260 U.S. 178 (1922).
37. "Japanese Given Citizenship for Service Lose It," *Sacramento Bee*, November 14, 1922, 1.
38. Harrod, "Jim Crow in the Navy."
39. "Steward to Four Presidents Dies."
40. Rachel Mason, "President Harding's Voyage of Understanding, June 1923," posted June 23, 2013, Alaska Historical Society website, www.alaskahistoricalsociety.org; "President Harding's Voyage of Understanding," White House Historical Association website, www.whitehousehistory.org.
41. June Allen, "A President's Ill-Fated Trip to Alaska," posted July 23, 2003, *Ketchikan Stories in the News*, reprinted in Mason, "President Harding's Voyage of Understanding."
42. Advertisement, *Washington Evening Star*, June 25, 1932, 28.
43. Advertisement, *Washington Evening Star*, August 27, 1932, 26.
44. "Steward to Four Presidents Dies."

CHAPTER TWO

The epigraph is from Lee Ping Quan, *To a President's Taste: Being the Reminiscences and Recipes of Lee Ping Quan, Ex-President's Steward on the Presidential Yacht, U.S.S. Mayflower, As Told to Jim Miller* (Emmaus, Pa.: Rodale Press, 1939), n.p., 30.

1. Ibid., 2.
2. Ibid.
3. "Lee Quan, Famed Navy Cook, Won Pershing, Coolidge Praise," *Brooklyn Daily Eagle*, January 18, 1943, 9.
4. Quan, *To a President's Taste*, 5.
5. Ibid., 7.
6. "Japanese Royalty Entertained Here," *Washington Evening Star*, November 8, 1925.
7. Quan, *To a President's Taste*, 9.
8. Ibid., 10.
9. Ibid., 20.
10. Ibid., 10–11.
11. Ibid., 11.
12. Barbara Marvin, "Mr. Quan Docks in New York," *Forecast Magazine*, June 1929, 381.
13. Ibid.; Quan, *To a President's Taste*, 12–13.
14. Quan, *To a President's Taste*, 15, 8.
15. Mildred Ann Smith, "What's Cooking? Rice Dishes for the Presidents," *Santa Cruz Sentinel*, July 12, 1972, 4.
16. Quan, *To a President's Taste*, 24.
17. Quoted in ibid., 25.
18. "Cooked for Presidents, Goes 'Broke' in N.Y.," *Lancaster (Pa.) Intelligencer Journal*, December 14, 1929, 3; "The Oracle," *Holyoke (Mass.) Transcript-Telegram*, July 6, 1929, 14.
19. "The Oracle."
20. "Lee Ping Quan's New Job," *Washington Evening Star*, April 19, 1929, 21.
21. Quan, *To a President's Taste*, 22–23.
22. Marvin, "Mr. Quan Docks in New York," 380.
23. Quan, *To a President's Taste*, 26.
24. Ibid., 26–27.
25. Ibid., 27.
26. Vance Griffith, "Once Cooked for Coolidge, Now Serves Multitudes," *Altoona (Pa.) Tribune*, August 19, 1929, 7, 11; "Cooked for Presidents, Goes 'Broke' in N.Y."
27. William Grimes, *Appetite City: A Culinary History of New York* (New York: North Point Press, 2009), 241; Seymour Deming, "Notes of Gotham," *Sioux City Journal*, April 26, 1930, 12.
28. "New York Skylines," *Atlanta Constitution*, February 20, 1938, 5K.
29. Advertisement in "Guide for Shoppers in Lincoln and Vicinity," *Bangor Daily News*, June 30, 1932, 11.
30. "New York Skylines."
31. Quan, *To a President's Taste*, 28.
32. US Inflation Calculator website, www.usinflationcalculator.com.
33. Quoted in "New York Skylines."
34. Quan, *To a President's Taste*, 28–29.
35. Ibid., 30.
36. "Lee Quan, Famed Navy Cook." See also Alex Prud'homme, "President Calvin Coolidge, Lee Ping Quan, and the Pleasures of a Floating Table," *White House History Quarterly*, no. 71 (Fall 2023): 52.
37. "Ex-Cook on *Mayflower* to Get Military Funeral," *Washington Star*, January 18, 1943, A-8.
38. "Lee Quan, Famed Navy Cook."
39. Kenneth T. Walsh, "Time on the Water: The Floating White House and the Presidents at Sea," *White House History Quarterly*, no. 71 (Fall 2023): 12.
40. Walter W. Jaffee, *The Presidential Yacht Potomac* (Palo Alto, Calif.: Glencannon Press, 1998), 40.
41. Ibid., 40–41.
42. Walsh, "Time on the Water," 12.
43. Ibid., 9.
44. "House Panel Considers Buying Back Presidential Yacht Sold by Carter," *Alexandria (Va.) Daily Town Talk*, May 2, 1978, C4.
45. Giles M. Kelly, *Sequoia: Presidential Yacht* (Centreville, Md.: Tidewater, 2004), x.
46. Ibid., 68.

CHAPTER THREE

The epigraph is from Melinda M. Dart, *A Glimpse of Greatness: The Memoir of Irineo Esperancilla* (2022), 63.

1. Melinda M. Dart, interview by author Adrian Miller on October 15, 2024, at the White House Historical Association, Washington, D.C. See also Melinda Dart, with Marcia Anderson, "Irineo Esperancilla, U.S. Navy Steward to Four Presidents: Faithful Service Remembered," *White House History Quarterly*, no. 70 (Summer 2023): 37–38.
2. Dart interview.
3. Dart, *Glimpse of Greatness*, 6.
4. Quoted in Lawrence L. Knutson, *Away from the White House: Presidential Escapes, Retreats, and Vacations* (Washington, D.C.: White House Historical Association, 2014), 220.
5. Ibid.
6. Ibid., 222.
7. Dart, *Glimpse of Greatness*, 8.
8. Knutson, *Away from the White House*, 222.
9. Dart, *Glimpse of Greatness*, 8–9.
10. Ibid., 13–14.
11. Knutson, *Away from the White House*, 245.
12. Dart, *Glimpse of Greatness*, 16.
13. Ibid., 17, 21, 22.
14. Ibid., 29–30.
15. Ibid., 51.
16. Ibid., 66.
17. Edward L. Beach, memorandum to Irineo Esperancilla, June 25, 1955, copy printed in Dart, *Glimpse of Greatness*, 68.
18. Ibid., 86.
19. Knutson, *Away from the White House*, 286, 292, 294.
20. Ibid., 302.
21. Ibid., 319–22.
22. Ibid., 336.
23. Ibid., 351–52.
24. Ibid., 367.
25. Ariel De Guzman, *The Bush Family Cookbook* (New York: Scribner, 2005), 7–8.
26. Ibid., 11.
27. J. B. West, with Mary Lynn Kotz, *Upstairs at the White House: My Life with the First Ladies* (New York: Coward, McCann & Geoghegan, 1973), 98–99.
28. Ibid., 123.
29. Ibid., 124.
30. Ibid.
31. De Guzman, *Bush Family Cookbook*, 18.
32. "Cheap White House Lunch," *Kingston (N.Y.) Daily Freeman*, December 2, 1974, 6.
33. Bradley H. Patterson Jr., *The White House Staff: Inside the West Wing and Beyond* (Washington, D.C.: Brookings Institution Press, 2000), 368–69.
34. Ibid., 369.
35. De Guzman, *Bush Family Cookbook*, 10–12.
36. Ibid., 256.
37. Ibid., 22.
38. Ibid., 23.
39. Ibid., 25.
40. Ibid., 161.
41. George H. W. Bush, foreword to ibid., [1].

CHAPTER FOUR

The epigraph is from an interview with Cristeta Comerford by author Adrian Miller on October 15, 2024, at the White House Historical Association in Washington, D.C.

1. Virginia W. Kelly, "Fine Chefs Considered Capital's Finest Jewels," *Honolulu Star-Bulletin*, March 10, 1961, 15; Lee Walsh, "'L'Affaire Bui' Quieting," *Washington Evening Star*, February 23, 1961, B8.
2. "Report of Marriage License Applications," *Washington Evening Star*, April 26, 1951, B2; "Obituaries," *Orlando Sentinel*, March 31, 1981, 4C.
3. Walsh, "'L'Affaire Bui' Quieting."
4. Ed Koterba, "A Bit of Washington," *Hammond (Ind.) Times*, December 13, 1957, B2; US Inflation Calculator website, www.usinflationcaculator.com.
5. Merriman Smith, "President Sick with Stomach Upset," *Contra Costa (Calif.) Gazette*, June 10, 1957, 1.
6. Lonnelle Aikman, "Inside the White House," *National Geographic* 119, no. 1 (June 1961): 34.
7. "Here's What Queen, Philip Ate at Dinner," *Atlanta Journal*, October 18, 1957, 6.
8. "White House Dinner Menu," *Buffalo News*, September 16, 1959, 16.
9. Sherman Adams, *Firsthand Report: The Story of the Eisenhower Administration* (New York: Harper & Brothers, 1961), 426–27.
10. Helen Thomas, "Fish Chowder Is Favorite Food of President," *Marion (Ind.) Chronicle Tribune*, March 2, 1961, 21.
11. Walsh, "'L'Affaire Bui' Quieting."
12. J. B. West, with Mary Lynn Kotz, *Upstairs at the White House: My Life with the First Ladies* (New York: Coward, McCann & Geoghegan, 1973), 328.
13. Ibid., 328–29.
14. William Seale, "The Matter of Rats in the White House," *White House History*, no. 43 (Fall 2016): 67, 72.
15. Quoted in Walsh, "'L'Affaire Bui' Quieting."
16. Ibid.
17. "Elsbeth R. Moss, Richard Wakefield Married at Fort Meyers, Va., Chapel," *Waterville (Maine) Morning Sentinel*, February 12, 1965, 3.
18. "Obituaries," *Orlando Sentinel*.
19. Unless otherwise cited, the content for this section and the quotations come from the Comerford interview.
20. Aishvarya Kavi, "Cristeta Comerford, White House Chef to 5 Presidents, Retires," *New York Times*, August 3, 2024.
21. Aishvarya Kavi, "Who Is White House Executive Chef Cristeta Comerford?" *National*, December 1, 2022.
22. Marian Burros, "First Woman Is Selected as Executive Chef at White House," *New York Times*, August 15, 2005.
23. Kavi, "Who Is White House Executive Chef Cristeta Comerford?"
24. Ibid.
25. Walter Scheib and Andrew Friedman, *White House Chef: Eleven Years, Two Presidents, One Kitchen* (Hoboken, N.J.: John Wiley & Son, 2007), 57.
26. Ibid., 296.
27. Ibid., 295–96.
28. Ibid., 296.
29. Burros, "First Woman Is Selected as Executive Chef at White House."
30. Kavi, "Who Is White House Executive Chef Cristeta Comerford?"
31. Quoted in Michelle Obama, *American Grown: The Story of the White House Kitchen Garden and Gardens Across America* (New York: Crown Publishers, 2012), 66–67.
32. Ibid., 241, 251; Jonathan Oosting, "Beer Lovers to Obama: Release Your White House Ale Recipe," *Grand Rapids Press*, September 6, 2012, 6.
33. Obama, *American Grown*, 68.
34. Quoted in Kavi, "Cristeta Comerford, White House Chef to 5 Presidents, Retires."

CHAPTER FIVE

The epigraph is from an interview with Permsin ("Tommy") Kurpradit by author Adrian Miller on December 7, 2024, at the Hotel Washington in Washington, D.C.

1. Melinda M. Dart, interview by author Adrian Miller, October 15, 2024, at the White House Historical Association, Washington, D.C.
2. The content for this section and the quotations come from an interview with Susan Limb by Adrian Miller on October 15, 2024, at the Praline Bakery & Bistro, Bethesda, Maryland.
3. For more on Chef Roland Mesnier's desserts, see his illustrated book *A Sweet World of White House Desserts* (Washington, D.C.: White House Historical Association, 2011).
4. Quoted in Caryn Rousseau, "Capital Culture: Obamas Invite Famous Guest Chefs," *Opelika-Auburn (Ala.) News*, February 5, 2010, 8C.
5. Quoted in ibid.
6. "About," Chef Anita Lo website, www.chefanitalo.com.
7. Anita Lo, account written for this book, August 6, 2024.
8. "Edward Lee," *Food*, PBS website, www.pbs.org.
9. Succotash website, www.succotash.com.
10. Banhisha Kundu, "'You're Still My Winner': 'Culinary Class Wars' Edward Lee Wins the Internet with His Endless Creative Skills and Diaspora Story," modified October 8, 2004, Sport Skeeda website, www.sportskeeda.com.
11. All these programs are described on the Chef Edward Lee website, www.chefedwardlee.com.
12. Edward Lee, account written for this book, December 3, 2024.
13. The content for this section and the quotations come from the Kurpradit interview.

Illustration Credits

All images are copyrighted by the White House Historical Association unless otherwise listed below and may not be reproduced without permission of the copyright owner.

AP	Associated Press
NARA	National Archives and Records Administration
LOC	Library of Congress
WH Photo	White House Photo

FRONT MATTER

xii–1	Courtesy of Melinda Dart

HISTORY

3	Newspapers.com
4	Getty Images
6	Getty Images
7	Getty Images
8	Japan-America Society of NH
9	LOC
11	LOC
12	LOC
13	Newspapers.com
16	LOC
17	Getty Images
19	Newspapers.com
21	*New York Sun*
22	Newspapers.com
25	Courtesy of Melinda Dart
27	Both: Courtesy of Melinda Dart
28	AP
30	Courtesy of Melinda Dart
31	Courtesy of Melinda Dart
33	AP
34	Getty Images
37	WH Photo
40	Shutterstock
42	Shutterstock
44	Getty Images
47	AP
49	Getty Images
50	Top: Bruce M. White for the White House Historical Association Bottom: Courtesy of Melinda Dart
51	George W. Bush Presidential Library and Museum
52	Collection of Roland Mesnier
54	Alamy Stock Photo
57	WH Photo
58	AP
59	WH Photo
61	WH Photo
62	Getty Images
63	WH Photo

RECIPES

All food photography is by Bruce M. White for the White House Historical Association, with the exception of photographs by Christina Hancock for the White House Historical Association on pages 115, 119, 147, and 161.

Stylist: Takako Kuniyuki

Propist: Christina Ewald

Recipes on pages 154–59 are from *The Bush Family Cookbook* by Ariel De Guzman. Copyright 2005 by Ariel De Guzman. Reprinted with permission of Scribner, an imprint of Simon & Schuster LLC. All rights reserved.

BACK MATTER

170	Ryan Fila
171	Courtesy of Deborah Chang

Index

Page numbers in *italics* indicate illustrations.

A
Adams, Sherman, 40–41
Allen, June, 10, 13
Almond Cookies, 114, *115*
Apple Fritters, 132
Arizona, USS, 26
Arrington, "Red," 41
Asaka, Nobuko, Princess (Japan), 18
Asaka, Yasuhiko, Prince (Japan), 18
Attea, Mary, *54*, 55
Augusta, USS, 29
Avocado and Citrus Salad with Endive, *84*, 85

B
Baldrige, Letitia, 41
Barbecue Saddle of Lamb, 102–103
Barry, USS, 16
Beach, Edward L., 31
Begin, Menachem, 31
Biden, Jill, 56, *58*, 59
Biden, Joe, 56, 59, *59*
Bonaparte, Charles Joseph, 7
Boulud, Daniel, 62
Braised Beef Short Ribs, 145
Bush, Barbara, 33–35
Bush, George H. W., ix, 32–35, *33*, 45
Bush, George W., 35, 45, 53
Bush, Jenna, 63
Bush, Laura, 45
Butter Bean Grits, 146, *147*
Butter-Poached Maine Lobster, 149

C
Camilla, Duchess of Cornwall, 45
Camp David (Shangri-La), 26, 28–31, *30*, 35
Camp Rapidan, 26
Carey, Lillie, 10
Carter, Jimmy, 23, 31, 47
Cauliflower Mac and Cheese, 160, *161*
Chaparral Wilted Spinach Salad, 154
Charles, Prince of Wales, *37*, 45
Chicken à la President, 73
Chicken and Rice Porridge, 93

Chicken Chow Mein, 106–108
Chicken Noodle Soup, 92
Chicken Stuffing in Mushrooms, 74
Chilled Yellow Squash Soup, 144
Chocolate Cookies, 118, *119*
Chocolate Cream Pie, *134*, 135–137
Chop Suey, Mrs. Coolidge's Favorite, 104, *105*
Chung, Ah, 6
Chung, Chew, 6
Churchill, Winston, ix, 28–29
Clam Chowder, 89
Clinton, Bill, x, 45, 53, 62
Clinton, Hillary, 45, 53
Collick, Adam, 46
Combination Sliced Vegetable Salad, 76
Comerford, Cristeta Pasia, ix, 36, *37*, 44, 44–47, *47*, 53, *54*, 58, *58*, 60, 62–63
Comerford, Danielle, 46
Comerford, John, 45, 46
Concord, USS, 26
Constitution, USS, 32
Coolidge, Calvin, ix, 7, *15*, *17*, 18–22, *19*
Coolidge, Grace, 2, 9, 19–22
Corn Fritters, 77
Creamed Cauliflower, 80
Crim, Howard, 32

D
Dart, Melinda, 26, 27, 31
De Guzman, Ariel, ix, 32–35, *33*, *34*
Decatur (torpedo boat), 23
Dennison, Robert L., 32
Despatch, USS, 5
Dolphin, USS, 5, *7*
Duck Chow Mein, à la Quan, 108, *109*

E
Egg Rolls, 70, *71*
Eggplant Croquettes, 81
Eisenhower, Dwight D., ix, 23, 29, 31, 39–43
Eisenhower, Mamie, *30*, 39–40, *40*, 42, *42*
Elizabeth II, Queen (Great Britain), 39–40
Esperancilla, Irineo, viii, ix, 24–31, *25*, *28*, *30*, *31*, 50
Esperancilla, Maryann, 26

F
Ficklin, Charles, *42*
Filet Mignon, 96, *97*
Ford, Gerald, 23, 31, 47
French Dressing, 88
Fried Green Asparagus Tips, 82, *83*
Fruit Muffins, 130
Fukuhara, Shiba, 6

G
Garlic Edamame Dumplings, 163
Gaui, Hoo, 6
Gorbachev, Mikhail, 35
Grayson, Cary T., 10
Grilled Loin of Lamb, 151

H
Haller, Henry, 47
Harding, Florence, 9, 18
Harding, Warren G., ix, 5, 9, 10, 13, 15–19, *16*
Harrison, Benjamin, 5
Harrison, Caroline, 42
Harrod, Frederick S., 7
Hayes, Rutherford B., 5
Heaton, Gen. and Mrs., 42
Hee, Ah, 6
Henderson, USS, 10, 13
Hilton, James, 26
Honey Fitz (yacht), 23
Hoover, Herbert, 5, 9, 20, 26, 31
Hu, Ah, 6
Hui, Haw, 6

J
Jaffee, Walter, 5
Jelly Roll, 126, *127*
Johnson, Lyndon Baines, 23, 31, 41, 47

K
Kaltman, Mary, 41
Kelly, Giles M., 23
Kennedy, Jacqueline, ix, 41
Kennedy, John F., 23, 31, 41
Khrushchev, Nikita, 40
Knutson, Lawrence L., 26
Komura Jutarō, *4*, 5–6
Kurpradit, Permsin ("Tommy"), ix, 48, *49*, 60–63, *61*, *62*, *63*

L

Laub, USS, 17
Lee, Edward, 56–59, *57, 58*
Lemon Dressing, 86
Lemon Icing, *124,* 125
Lemon Squall, 138, *139*
Limb, Susan, ix, *51,* 51–53, *52,* 63
Lincoln, Abraham, 5, 26
Lincoln, Mary Todd, 39
Liu, Fong, 6
Lo, Anita, *54,* 54–55
London Pound Cake, 122, *123*
Long, John D., 5
Loy, Ah, 2, *3,* 6–9, *9*
Lung, Ah, 6
Lynch, Jack, 23

M

Makino, Hsaio, 5
Mandela, Nelson, 45
Maryland Crab Cakes, *142,* 143
Masak, Chinoski, 5
Masaki, Cho, 5
Matsudaira, Tsuneo, 18
Mayflower, USS, ix, xi, *4,* 5–11, *6, 8, 9,* 15–22, *16, 17, 19,* 26
McCartin, Lynn, *51*
McKinley, William, 5, 6
McLaurin, Stewart D., *viii,* ix
Mesnier, Roland, 51, *51,* 53
Miami (revenue cutter), 5
Miller, Jim, xi, 5, 16, 18, 20, 22
Moeller, John, 60, 62
Morrison, Susan, *51,* 53, *54, 58*
Mrs. Coolidge's Favorite Chop Suey, 104, *105*
Musel, Patrick, *51,* 53
Mushroom Soup, 150

N

Nimitz, Chester W., 23
Nixon, Richard, 23, 31, 47
Noa, USS, 26

O

Oatmeal Cookies, 116
Obama, Barack, 46, 53–55
Obama, Michelle, 46–47, 53–55, *54*
O'Connell, Patrick, 62
Oka, Fukusa, 5
Okida, Tsukasa, 6
Ono, Sorzavola, 6
Orange Marmalade Muffins, 131

P

Paje, Juanito ("Johnny"), 50, *50*
Palustra, Ambrucio, 10
Pancit, 162
Patterson, Bradley H., Jr., 32–33
Peach Muffins, *128,* 129
Peanut Cookies, 117

Peng Liyuan, 54–55
Pershing, John J., 18
Philip, Prince (Great Britain), 39–40
Poppy Seed Bread and Butter Pudding, 152, *153*
Pork Adobo, *158,* 159
Potomac, USS, *viii,* 23, 28, *28*
Prayut Chan-o-cha, 63
President Coolidge's Rice and Curry, 98
Puffed Cheese Rolls, 155

Q

Quan, Lee Ping, ix, xi, 14–23, *15, 19, 21,* 67

R

Ramsdell, Mark, 53
Reagan, Ronald, 31, 33, 47
Rendon, Paula, 35
Rice and Curry, President Coolidge's, 98
River Queen (paddle steamer), 5
Rochemont, Helen de Bogart de, 20
Rochemont, Louis de, 20
Roosevelt, Edith, 7–8, 26
Roosevelt, Eleanor, 28
Roosevelt, Franklin D., viii, ix, 23, 25, 26, *28,* 28–29
Roosevelt, Theodore, ix, *4,* 4–8
Rosen, Roman Romanovich, *4,* 5, 7
Rostang, Michel, 54
Roudebush, Marlene, *51*
Row, Yoji, 6
Russian Dressing, 87
Russo-Japanese War, ix, *4,* 4–8, 10
Rysavy, François, 39

S

Sadat, Anwar, 31
Samuelsson, Marcus, 53, 54
Sato, Kisogee, 5
Savoy, Guy, 54
Scheib, Walter, 45, 62
Seale, William, 42
Sequoia, USS, 23, 28
Sherrill, C. O., 10
Shoestring Potatoes, 78, *79*
Shrimp à la *Mayflower,* 72
Sigand/Sigando, Marguerite/Margaritta, 10
Singh, Manmohan, 53
Snyder, Howard McCrum, 39
Sorghum-Glazed Carrots, 148
Spanish-American War, 5
Stalin, Joseph, ix, 28–29
Steamed Boneless Fish, 99
Strawberry à la King Pie, 133
Strawberry Shortcake, 121
Sun, Li Wan, 16
Sylph, USS, 5

T

Takahira Kogorō, *4,* 6
Tartar Dressing, 88
Thomas, Helen, 41
Tomato Cream Soup, 90, *91*
Tricolor Pepper Steak, *110,* 111
Truman, Bess, 32
Truman, Harry S., 23, 29, 31, *31,* 32
Trump, Donald J., 63, *63*
Tsurusaki, Shiro, ix, 10–13, *11, 12*

U

Udo, Pedro, ix, *38,* 39–43, *40, 42, 43*

V

Van Han, Bui, 41
Vanilla Almond Cookies, 120
Verdon, René, 41

W

Walsh, Kenneth T., 5, 23
Watanabe, Masa, 6
Way, Chiu, 6
West, J. B., 32, 41–42
White House Cheese Blisters, 156, *157*
White House Fried Chicken, 100, *101*
White House Fried Shrimp, 75
Williamsburg, USS, 23, 29, 31, 32
Wilson, Woodrow, 9
Wing, Ah, 6
Witte, Sergei, *4,* 5–6
Wong, Ah, 6
World War I, 10, 16, 18
World War II, ix, 23, 28–29
Wright, Orville, 13
Wright, Wilbur, 13

X

Xi Jinping, 54–55

Y

Yawada, Jutaro, 5
Yeren, Jeannete, 39
Yesaki, Yukichi, 5
Ying, Hung, 6
Yoon Suk Yeol, 56, 58, 59, *59*
Yosemite, USS, 39
Yue, Ing Yee, 6

About the Author
ADRIAN MILLER

Adrian Miller is a food writer and attorney. A two-time James Beard Award winner, he is the author of *Soul Food: The Surprising Story of an American Cuisine, One Plate at a Time*; *The President's Kitchen Cabinet: The Story of the African Americans Who Have Fed Our First Families, From the Washingtons to the Obamas*; and *Black Smoke: African Americans and the United States of Barbecue*. He received his AB in international relations from Stanford University in 1991 and a JD from the Georgetown University Law Center in 1995. In 2022, he was awarded an honorary doctorate from the Denver Institute for Urban Studies and Adult College. From 1999 to 2001, Miller served as a special assistant to President Bill Clinton with his Initiative for One America and went on to serve as a senior policy analyst for Colorado Governor Bill Ritter Jr. Since 2013, Miller has been the executive director of the Colorado Council of Churches. He is also the co-project director and lead curator for the "Proclaiming Colorado's Black History" exhibit at the Museum of Boulder. A certified barbecue judge, Miller lives in Denver, Colorado.

About the Author
DEBORAH CHANG

After graduating from the Napa Valley Culinary School, Deborah Chang cooked at numerous Bay Area restaurants, created award-winning recipes for Diamond Crystal Kosher Salt and the National Peanut Board. Chang was born and raised in a suburb of Detroit, Michigan, where she remembers routinely heading over to Windsor, Canada, to enjoy *jing du* pork chops, lugging Chinese groceries back across the border, and wondering why almond chicken was the most popular dish at her parents' restaurant, Dragon Inn. She is a graduate of Stanford University and the University of Michigan Law School. Her expansive career has included being an attorney, a tech executive, and most recently a career counselor. Chang's writings have been published in the *San Francisco Chronicle*, the *Hill*, and Bridge Eight Literary Press. She now resides in the San Francisco Bay Area with her husband and two daughters.

Acknowledgments

A big thank you to the following people who immeasurably helped with this project: Jennifer L. Cook, for great editing of the early manuscript, and the staff at the Dwight D. Eisenhower Presidential Library and the National Archives. A special thank you to Stewart D. McLaurin, Marcia Anderson, Lauren McGwin, and Matthew Costello of the White House Historical Association for believing in this project. As always, I thank my friends and family for your continued support, and God for blessing me with the opportunity to share these stories with the world.—Adrian Miller

One of the best parts of this project was working with Chef Scot Rice and his students at Florian High School in Sacramento. Chef Scot and I went to Napa Culinary School together and graduated in 2003. I was able to see how much he has mastered his craft in the last twenty years during this project. Thank you to him and his students, in no particular order: Yair Gonzalez, John, Nick, Messi, Josue Martinez, Rubi Lopez, Valeri, Dean, Kirk, Christopher Yang, Raihana Suttani, Faizel, Djeffterline Jean Philippe, Shawn Cha, Alvin Singh, Lucas Lee, Axel Ocha, Anthony Cross, Valeva, Kaliyah Lee, Kim Hernandez, Ruby Chavez, Allison Vang, Aaliyah Lewis, Aneesa, Benji M, Jahien Garcia, Annabelle, Gia Lam, Jenny Yang, Leilani Carrasco, Alana Nkaujnag Lao, Emily Vue, Dillan Xiang, Stevin Xiong, Benji M, Natalia De La Cruz, Jahliem G., Jasmine Reyes, Paris, Skylar Yang, Zong Xiong, Alexander Gutierus, Rishe Ram, Yiwong Li, John Nguyen, Travis Lynch, Bahar, Amy, Alineh, Alan Chung, Juan, Cabrera, Daniel Zheng, Vincent Vang, Kyla, Dulce, Naoimi, Jocelyn, Kris Lim, Karina Ocampo, Edgar, Martin, Marcus, and Kyle. Thank you to Angie Ha, and my family, Chris, Chloe, and Maddy, for their support, as always.—Deborah Chang